Now you have a choice.

JN428975

Grammar-Based English

Tries to prevent 10,000 grammar mistakes,
and then measures your ability by how many mistakes you make.

Conversation Based Learning

Is all conversations and conversation tests. Find and fix your own mistakes.

Life is a contest of passion and ability.
This book will give you the ability to express your passion, in English.

Any questions?

CONTENTS

Scan the QR code for the Audio

The **WEBSITE** also has **Instruction Videos** and **MS Word Templates** for the **Paragraphs**, **Essays** and **Test Transcripts.**

WritingforSpeaking.com

Conversation Based Learning

1 Placement Test

Gives your ability, and your first test partners.

Placement Test Score	First Test Partners
99	
92	1
90	
89	
88	2
87	
85	
83	3
80	
79	
78	4
76	
73	
72	5
68	
67	
64	6
58	
57	
57	7
54	

2 Homework

Prepares you to speak, and it's 40% of your grade. *Do it.*

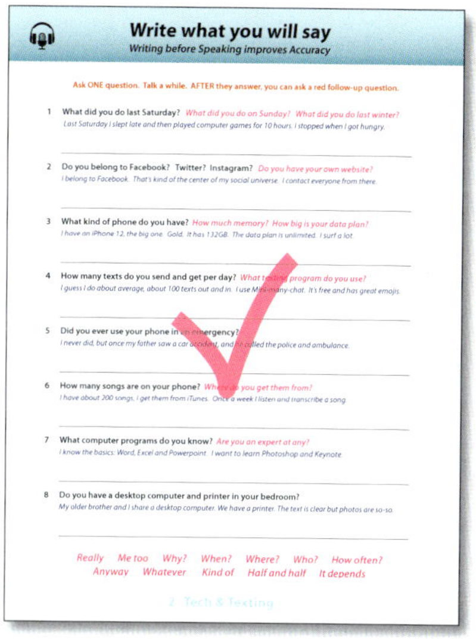
Write what you will say
Writing before Speaking improves Accuracy

Ask ONE question. Talk a while. AFTER they answer, you can ask a red follow-up question.

1 What did you do last Saturday? *What did you do on Sunday? What did you do last winter?*
Last Saturday I slept late and then played computer games for 10 hours. I stopped when I got hungry.

2 Do you belong to Facebook? Twitter? Instagram? *Do you have your own website?*
I belong to Facebook. That's kind of the center of my social universe. I contact everyone from there.

3 What kind of phone do you have? *How much memory? How big is your data plan?*
I have an iPhone 12, the big one. Gold. It has 132GB. The data plan is unlimited. I surf a lot.

4 How many texts do you send and get per day? *What t[illegible] program do you use?*
I guess I do about average, about 100 texts out and in. I use M[illegible]ny-chat. It's free and has great emojis.

5 Did you ever use your phone in [illegible]ergency?
I never did, but once my father saw a car [illegible], and [illegible]lled the police and ambulance.

6 How many songs are on your phone? *Wh[illegible] you get them from?*
I have about 200 songs. I get them from iTunes. On[illegible] a week I listen and transcribe a song.

7 What computer programs do you know? *Are you an expert at any?*
I know the basics: Word, Excel and Powerpoint. I want to learn Photoshop and Keynote.

8 Do you have a desktop computer and printer in your bedroom?
My older brother and I share a desktop computer. We have a printer. The text is clear but photos are so-so.

Really Me too Why? When? Where? Who? How often?
Anyway Whatever Kind of Half and half It depends

2 Tech & Texting

3 Conversation Class

Speed Dating.

One topic, many partners. *Fun.*

4 Conversation Test

3 students, 17 minutes.
Students record and transcribe.

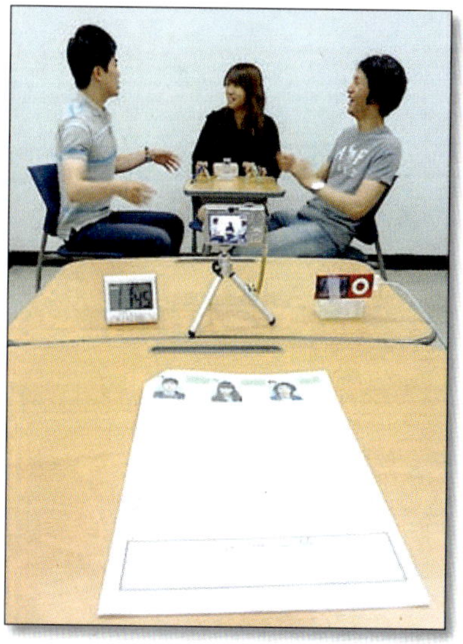

5 Transcript

Type just what you said.
Fix your own mistakes. *Simple.*

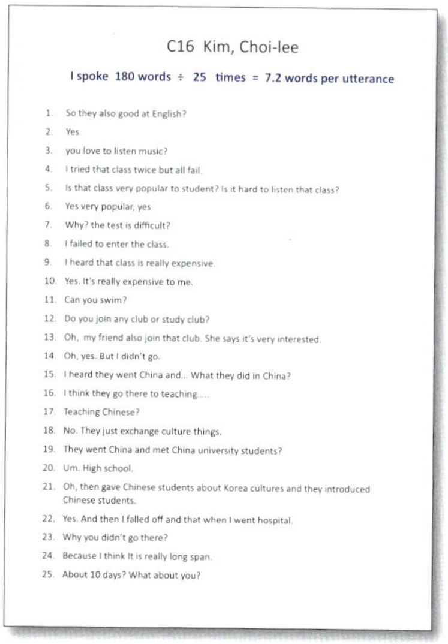
C16 Kim, Choi-lee

I spoke 180 words ÷ 25 times = 7.2 words per utterance

1. So they also good at English?
2. Yes
3. you love to listen music?
4. I tried that class twice but all fail.
5. Is that class very popular to student? Is it hard to listen that class?
6. Yes very popular, yes
7. Why? the test is difficult?
8. I failed to enter the class.
9. I heard that class is really expensive.
10. Yes. It's really expensive to me.
11. Can you swim?
12. Do you join any club or study club?
13. Oh, my friend also join that club. She says it's very interested.
14. Oh, yes. But I didn't go.
15. I heard they went China and... What they did in China?
16. I think they go there to teaching.....
17. Teaching Chinese?
18. No. They just exchange culture things.
19. They went China and met China university students?
20. Um. High school.
21. Oh, then gave Chinese students about Korea cultures and they introduced Chinese students.
22. Yes. And then I falled off and that when I went hospital.
23. Why you didn't go there?
24. Because I think It is really long span.
25. About 10 days? What about you?

6 Ability

The 1st test gives your ability, and your 2nd test partners.

	Total Words Spoken	Second Test Partners
	662	
A	649	1
	621	
	582	
	569	2
B	552	
	549	
	523	3
	518	
	451	
	427	4
	423	
C	360	
	341	5
	314	
	291	
D	254	6
	225	
	172	
D-	140	7
	129	

After midterm, do it again.

A comparison of midterm and final test data will show 50% improvement.

50% Improvement

	How many times I spoke	Average words per utterance	Total words I spoke
Practice test	40	10	400
Final test	26	18	480
Improvement		**80%**	**20%**

This book is different

1 The goal is smoother speaking

The one true goal of learning a foreign language is speaking ability. Life is a contest of passion and ability. This book will give you the ability to express your passion, in English.

2 Writing is speaking preparation

Your writing will not be corrected, so relax and ***write what interests you.***
Every question in the book is about you, so you know the answers. ***This book is all about you.***

3 This book uses repetition

All human learning can be summed up in three words: ***watch, try, repeat.***
Speaking is a skill. Skills are improved by repetitive practice. Repetition is the methodology.

4 This book uses pronunciation

The goal is smoother speaking, and for this, pronunciation is way more important than grammar. Every page is on audio. **Listen, repeat, record, and listen to yourself.** When you record, put some feeling into it. **Your voice *is* your personality.**

5 You get both Speaking Ability and Standardized Test Scores

How? ***Listening, reading, writing, vocabulary,*** and ***pronunciation*** are ***speaking*** preparation, and also improve. All examples are perfect ***grammar***, and that improves. When all those skills improve, so do **TOEIC, TOEFL** and **IELTS** scores. ***Simple***.

This book has a wire spine. *Why?*
It's a conversation book.

Conversation is the goal, the class, and the test. There is no smaller unit.

Simple.

We use partners, not grammar

This is the Class

The class is pair conversations. ***Speed Dating.***
You get a new topic every 2 weeks, a new partner every 7 minutes.
Everybody's speaking half the time, and half the time your partner's a better speaker.

This is the Test

Three students of similar ability have a 17-minute conversation.
Record it with your phone, transcribe just what you said, and self-correct.
The first test measures your ability, the second test measures your improvement.

The rest is details.

Conversation Class: *Speed Dating*

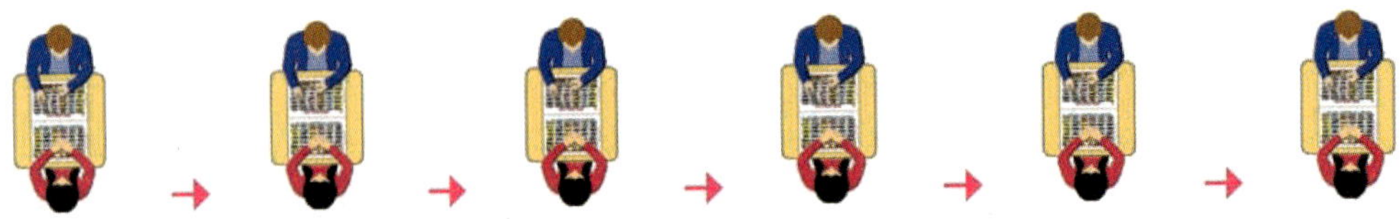

One topic, many partners

A new topic every week, a new partner every 7 minutes

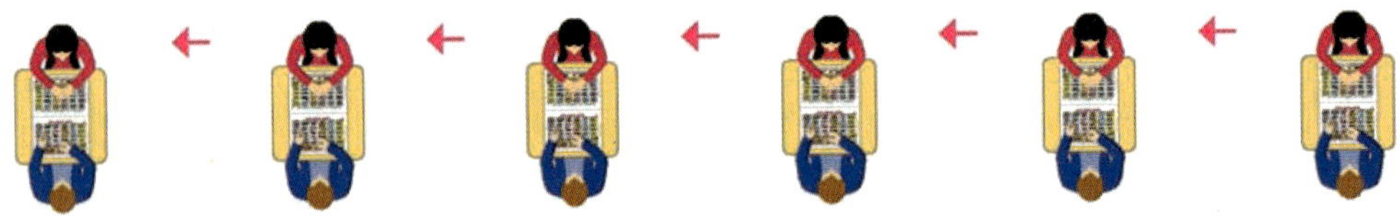

The bigger the class the better.

More partners = more variety = more interesting = more repetition = more improvement

1. Walk in, put your phone on the roll sheet, look at the board, find your seat and partner, and sit.
2. Meet, greet, introduce yourself, and chat. After 7 minutes, the teacher yells, ***SWITCH!***
3. Students seated on the inside say, ***Bye, Gotta go, Nice meeting you, See you later***, and move on.
4. Next class you'll do it again, better, smoother, with new partners.

We don't give you new grammar to study every week. ***We give you new partners!*** THEY provide you with new information, pronunciation, vocabulary, and questions. We don't give you advanced topics (not relevant and not interesting), we give you advanced ways to talk about yourself (very interesting).

How do you get good at something? *You do it more than once.*

Conversation Test

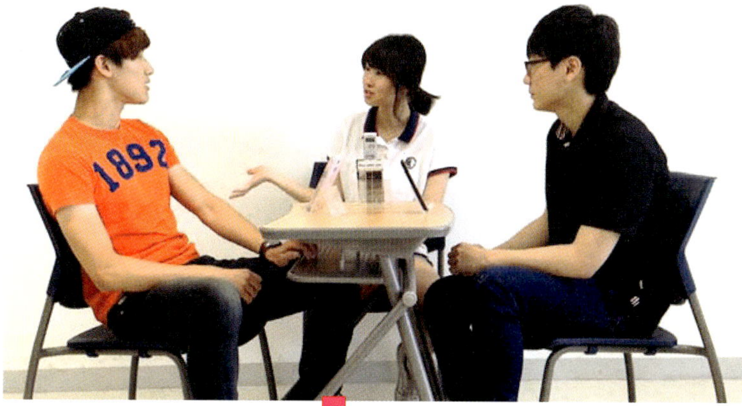

1. Three students of similar ability have a 17-minute conversation.
2. Record the conversation with your phone.
3. Transcribe what you said on MS Word. (about 90 minutes)
4. MS Word gives your speaking ability data!
5. It counts how many words you spoke, and how many times you spoke.
6. *Wow.*

Two hours after the test, you can email this to your teacher.

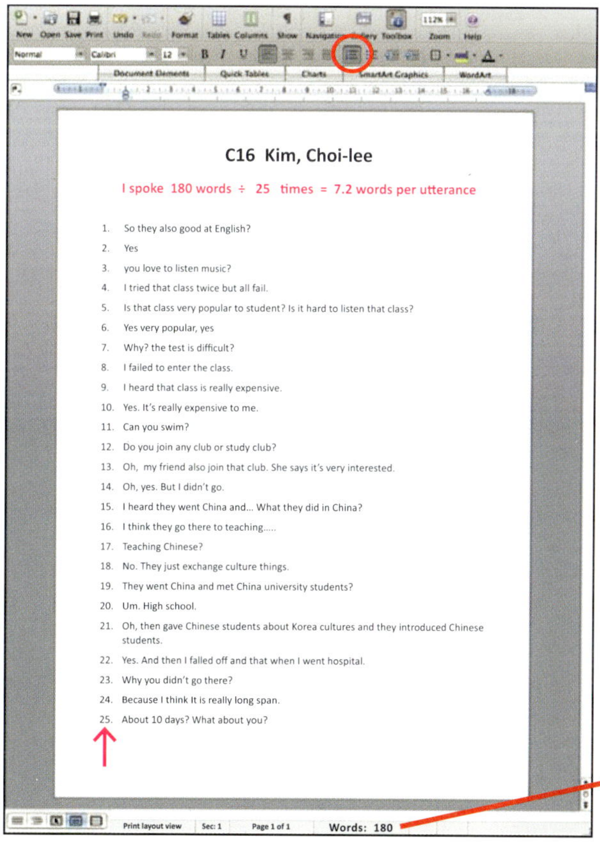

C16 Kim, Choi-lee

I spoke 180 words ÷ 25 times = 7.2 words per utterance

1. So they also good at English?
2. Yes
3. you love to listen music?
4. I tried that class twice but all fail.
5. Is that class very popular to student? Is it hard to listen that class?
6. Yes very popular, yes
7. Why? the test is difficult?
8. I failed to enter the class.
9. I heard that class is really expensive.
10. Yes. It's really expensive to me.
11. Can you swim?
12. Do you join any club or study club?
13. Oh, my friend also join that club. She says it's very interested.
14. Oh, yes. But I didn't go.
15. I heard they went China and... What they did in China?
16. I think they go there to teaching.....
17. Teaching Chinese?
18. No. They just exchange culture things.
19. They went China and met China university students?
20. Um. High school.
21. Oh, then gave Chinese students about Korea cultures and they introduced Chinese students.
22. Yes. And then I falled off and that when I went hospital.
23. Why you didn't go there?
24. Because I think It is really long span.
25. About 10 days? What about you?

Words: 180

	Total words spoken
1	695
2	668
3	643
4	582
5	564
6	544
7	521
8	509
9	453
10	421
11	421
12	398
13	367
14	345
15	321
16	288
17	267
18	245
19	180
20	167
21	149

There it is. *After 10 years of English education, and two hours after the test, the speaking ability of everyone in the class is known.*

Total words spoken on the first test determines partners for the second test.

Wow. Partners of similar ability. This will be fair, and accurate.

OH, THIS IS AWESOME!

1. Instead of studying grammar for 3 hours before the test, you transcribe for 1.5 hours after the test.
2. You ***hear*** and ***see*** your mistakes. ***Your teacher does not have to point them out.***
3. Word does all the data for you. How many words you speak is an accurate measure of your ability.
4. The midterm test shows your ability, and the final test shows your improvement.

Each unit has 12 pages. Do the book at home and speak in class.

1 Warm Up and Conversation Rehearsal

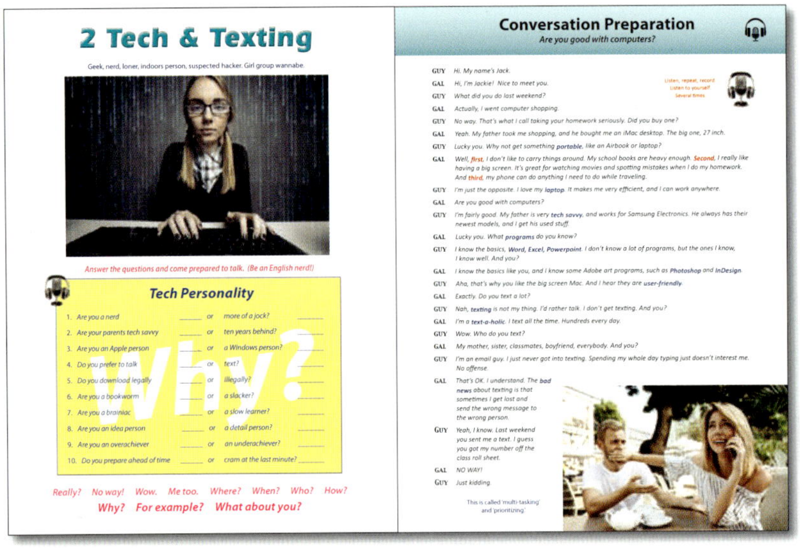

Page 1 Warm up

Listen, read, pronounce, and put checks in the blanks.

Get in the habit of asking ***For example?*** and ***What about you?***

Page 2 Model Conversation

Close the book, listen to the audio and repeat. Open the book, listen, read and repeat again. If you really want to improve, record and listen to yourself.

2 Get smoother at the Basics

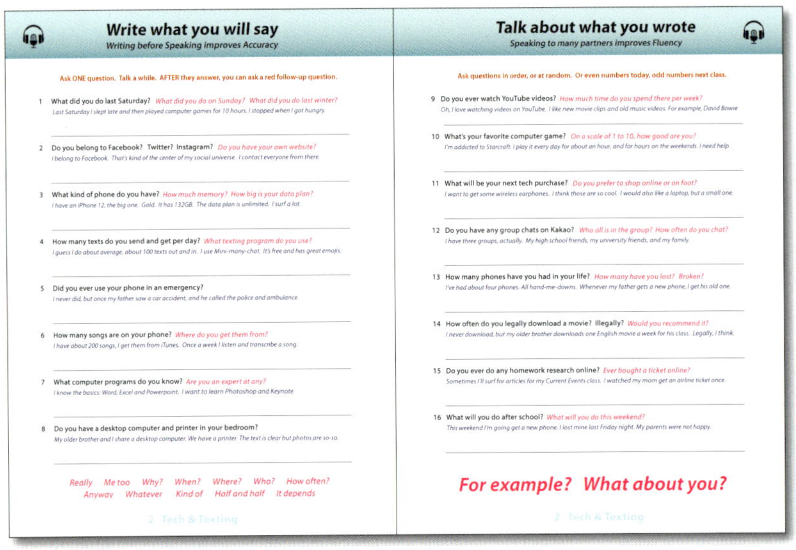

Pages 3 - 4 Write it, then say it

There are 16 conversation questions with example answers. Write your own answers and use them in class.

Always ask #1 first. It's always about last weekend. Then, ask questions in order or at random. When a conversation starts, go with it.

The last question is always about this weekend.

3 Add in some Vocabulary

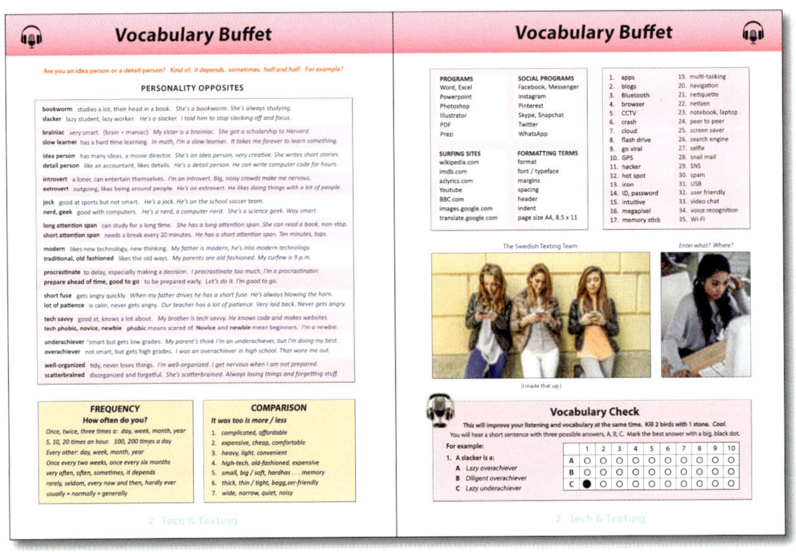

Pages 5 - 6 Vocabulary Buffet

It's a buffet. Don't try to memorize them all. Find 5 to 10 vocabulary and idioms that help describe your life.

Page 6 Vocabulary Listening Quiz

Take the quiz in the book, or even better, transcribe the quiz on MS Word and then answer it. While you're transcribing, you can look at the pages in the book and check your spelling.

Write what you will say, talk about what you wrote. *Simple.*

4 Longer, Smoother Speaking, and Pronunciation Practice

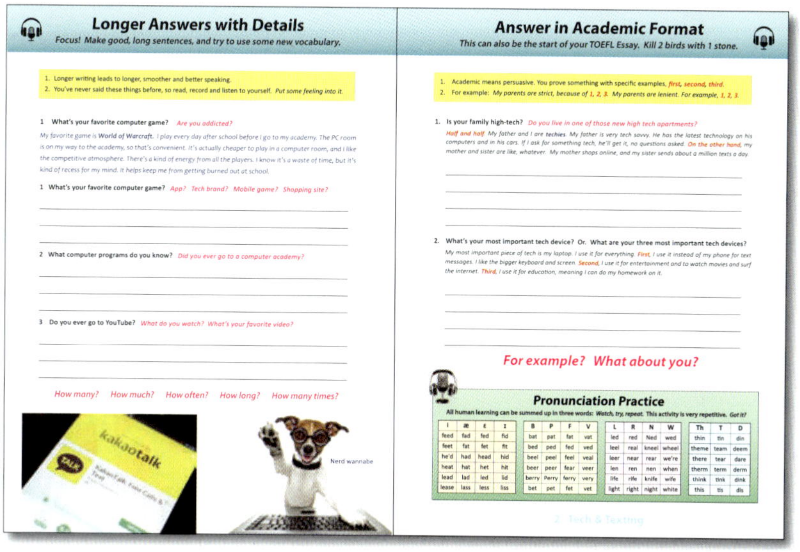

Page 7 Longer answers with details

Write longer answers, using details that you easily know: ***Where, when, who, why, how, how often, how long***.

Page 8 Answer in Academic Format

Answer with ***first, second, third,*** and use ***specific examples*** from your life.

Pronunciation Practice

Each audio is about 3 minutes, so you can practice 3 times in 10 minutes.

5 It's your life. Give specific details.

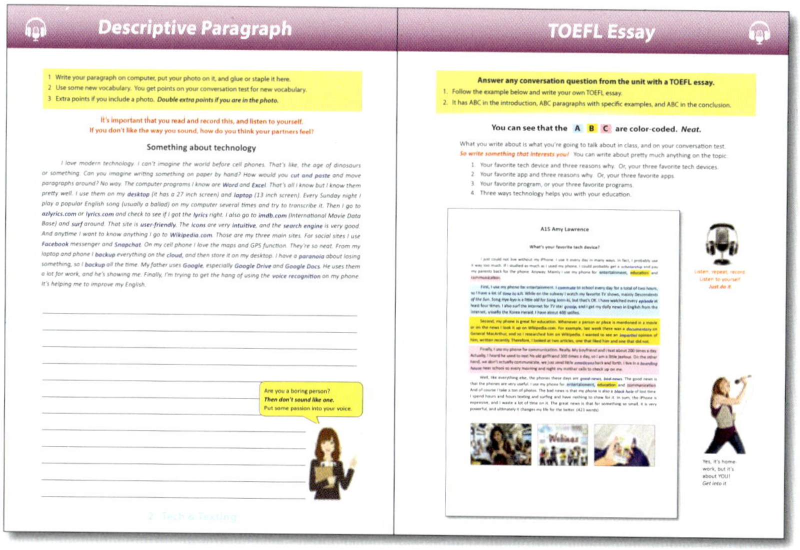

Page 9 Descriptive Paragraph

You can write in the book, but you will improve more if you write on a computer. It will check your spelling and grammar. *Cool.*

Page 10 TOEFL Essay

Answer any question in the unit (or make your own) in ABC, academic format. Use new vocabulary and specific examples from your life.

Read, record and listen. (This is great preparation for your conversation test.)

6 Do it again, better, with new partners

Pages 11 - 12 Wrap Party

Questions are colored by topic, and many are a little advanced. They require longer and more thoughtful answers. Ask questions at random or by topic.

There's usually a list for you to fill in. This can also be used to ask questions and start conversations.

You'll have longer and more interesting conversations, with new partners, using what you learned in the unit.

But first,

CONVERSATION ETIQUETTE

Every time you meet a new partner:

1. Introduce yourself. ***Hi. My name is James Bond. Hello, I'm James Bond.***
   Do not say, ***What's your name?*** This is a conversation, not a police interrogation.
2. Ask about the basics: ***What did you do last weekend? Where do you live? Do you have a hobby? What will you do after school today?*** Things like that.
3. When you change partners, say things like: ***Bye. Nice meeting you. This was fun. Later. See you later. Gotta go. Let's have lunch sometimes.***
4. After you answer a question, always, ALWAYS, ***ALWAYS*** ask, ***WHAT ABOUT YOU?***

#1 CONVERSATION SKILL: Follow-up questions

Every time your partner answers a question, ask some follow-up questions.

Where? When? Why? Who? How? How long? How often? What time?

With follow-up questions the conversation can go on forever. The longer you talk, the more you improve. (And, you can keep your partner talking until you figure out how to answer in English.)

#2 CONVERSATION SKILL: Comments

1. I DON'T UNDERSTAND	*Excuse me Again please Louder please Say what?*
2. AGREE	*Me too I hear that Ditto Absolutely*
3. DISAGREE	*Say what? Excuse me? No way You're kidding In your dreams*
4. THAT'S GREAT	*Wow Really? No kidding Cool Neat Congratulations You're the man*
5. THAT'S TOO BAD	*I'm sorry to hear that That's a shame That's terrible Bummer*
6. SORRY ABOUT THAT	*My bad Oops My mistake Sorry about that (you're just a little sorry)*
7. YOU'RE WELCOME	*My pleasure Anytime Don't mention it*
8. HURRY UP	*Chop chop Cut to the chase Shake a leg*
9. PRIVACY	*No comment That's personal That's none of your business*
10. CHANGE THE TOPIC	*Anyway Whatever*
PARTIAL ANSWERS	*Kind of Sort of It depends Half and half Sometimes*

ACADEMIC SKILLS: First, second, third, and specific examples

Here are the eight words you will say most often this semester:

What about you? For example? First, second, third

When you are asked "For example?" give **specific examples**. Giving specific examples is academic.

Academic means persuasive. It proves a point. *Nuclear power is good, (or bad) because of 1, 2, 3.* ***Avengers*** *is my favorite movie because of 1, 2, 3. Last weekend was awesome because of 1, 2, 3.*

A book gives specific examples with charts, data, and photos. You'll give specific examples from your life. You're the world's expert on you, so your specific examples are easy. Learn how to say them in English.

Instruction Conversation

You'll understand the class and improve your speaking. *Cool.* Kill two birds with one stone.

Speed Dating. Get ready to have 23 new friends.

GUY *Hi. I'm Jackson Lee.*

GAL *Hi. I'm Amy Lawrence. Nice to meet you.*

GUY *I missed class last week. Can you fill me in? How does this class work?*

GAL *It's pretty simple. Do the book at home and talk in class.*

GUY *That's it?*

GAL *That's it.*

GUY *What about grading?*

GAL *Well,* ***first****, it's a conversation class so there are conversation tests.* ***Second****, all we do is talk, but we must show up prepared to talk. And* ***third****, homework is about 40% of the grade, so be sure to do the book at home.*

GUY *That's fair. What are the classes like?*

GAL *Just like this. We sit in pairs and have conversations. We switch partners every seven minutes.*

GUY *Cool.*

GAL *Yeah. With pair conversations, everybody is speaking half the time, and half the time your partner is a better speaker.*

GUY *That's pretty smart.*

GAL *Yeah. And sometimes we sit in groups of three and have longer conversations. This adds variety and we can go into more detail.*

GUY *I can do that. What are the tests like?*

GAL *The conversation test is just like the class. Three students have a 15-minute conversation. We record it with our phones, and then transcribe it.*

GUY *How long does that take?*

GAL *About an hour and a half. By transcribing, we can hear and see our own mistakes. The good news is, during test week, we only come to class for the 15-minute test. Otherwise, we're free. FREE!*

GUY *Wow. I like that. So that's it? Conversations in class and a conversation test?*

GAL *Yep. That's it. The book provides the preparation, class provides the practice, and the test provides the error correction.*

GUY *Cool. When do we start?*

GAL *We already did. We're having a conversation. Get it?*

GUY *Got it. Oh, there's the bell. Now what?*

GAL *We switch partners. Bye bye. Nice meeting you.*

1. Listen & repeat
2. Listen & record
3. Listen to yourself

Several times

TOP 40 FIRST-DAY QUESTIONS

Introduce yourself. Ask any question. Talk a while, ask ***For example? What about you?*** Ask follow-up questions. Do not ask three questions back-to-back!

What's your major?
Do you like your major? What's your dream major?

What did you do last weekend?
Where? How long did you stay? What time did you get home?

Where do you live?
How long have you lived there? Where's your hometown?

How do you get to school?
How long does it take? Do you have a driver's license?

Do you belong to a club?
Is it a club in your major? How many are in the club?

How many text messages do you send per day?
How many do you get? Who do you send the most to?

Who's your favorite English language movie star?
Who's your favorite male star? Female star? Foreign star?

Are you a couch potato? (Do you watch TV all the time?)
Do you ever exercise? How many hours do you watch TV on the weekends?

How were your grades last semester?
Were you ever a class leader? Did you ever get a scholarship?

Do you look more like your father or mother?
How exactly? Are you taller than your mother? Your father?

How many universities did you apply to?
What school was your first choice? Did you stay out a year to study?

What does your father do? What does your mother do?
What exactly does he / she do? Do they work much at home?

Are you a morning person or an evening person?
What time do you usually wake up? What time do you usually go to sleep?

How often do you exercise?
What exercise? Do you belong to a health club? Do your parents belong?

What do you usually do on the weekends?
Do you use the weekends to study, rest or hang out with your friends?

Who's your favorite singer or group?
Who's your favorite member? Can you sing? Are you a good dancer?

Are you skilled at anything? Music, art, sports, sleeping?
Did you ever win a contest? Olympic gold medal? Gotten a scholarship?

Are your parents strict or lenient?
Who's more strict, your father or mother? They're strict about what?

Are you close to your brother (or sister)?
Do you confide in them, or keep secrets? What's the age gap?

What will you do tonight? What will you do this weekend?
On Saturday or Sunday? What time do you wake up on Sunday?

Really? Me too! Where? When? Why? Who? How often? Kind of Half and half It depends

For example? WHAT ABOUT YOU?

Hi. My name's ____________ What did you do last summer?

Introduce yourself. Ask any question. Talk a while, ask ***For example? What about you?*** Ask follow-up questions. Do not ask three questions back-to-back!

Where were you born?
How long have you lived there? Did your family move many times?

What high school did you go to?
What was your favorite subject in high school? Why? Your least favorite?

What did you do last summer / winter vacation?
How long did you stay? Who did you go with? Would you go again?

Do you ever watch YouTube?
What kinds of videos? Who's your favorite YouTube personality?

Do your parents give you an allowance?
How much? Is it enough? Do you get money on your birthday?

What time is your curfew? (When you must return home at night.)
What's the latest that you ever got home? Were you punished?

What's your favorite sport or exercise?
Do you like to play sports, or just watch them? How often do you exercise?

Do you play a musical instrument?
How long have you played? How old were you when you started?

What was your easiest subject last semester?
What was your hardest? Do you have a free day this semester?

Are you good with computers?
What programs do you know? What's your favorite computer game?

What's your dream job? What's your Plan B? Plan C?
Did you take a gap year? How many? Where did you study?

Did you ever have a part-time job?
How often did you work? How was the pay? Were you ever a tutor?

What's your favorite TV show?
When does it come on? Who are the stars? Why do you like it?

Do you have a hobby?
When did you start? Do you belong to a club? How do you relax?

How many phones have you had in your life?
Did you ever lose a phone? Did you ever use your phone in an emergency?

What's your favorite western food?
Do you prefer Chinese or Japanese food? Do you cook?

Have you ever traveled abroad?
How many countries have you been to? Which one was your favorite?

Who's your favorite movie star? Male star? Female star?
How often do you watch an English movie? Where usually?

Are you more like your father or mother? (more similar to)
Why? Do your parents have similar personalities? Are they opposites?

Did you make any new friends last semester?
Are they friends in your major? Did you make any enemies?

Really? Me too! Where? When? Why? Who? How often? Kind of Half and half It depends

For example? WHAT ABOUT YOU?

Do you belong to a club?

3 The first group to finish makes an F.
If you finish quickly, it means you're not asking follow-up questions.

Start

- Do you belong to a club?
- What's your favorite TV show?
- Do you have a hobby? Did you ever win a contest?
- What did you do last weekend? Last night?
- Who's your favorite movie star?
- Did you ever travel abroad?
- Where do you live? Where were you born?
- What did you do last summer/winter vacation?
- What's your favorite computer game?
- What's your favorite food? What food do you hate?
- What was your best subject in high school? Your worst?

keep going

that way

- Did you ever go to a pop music concert?
- What's your schedule this semester?
- Are you close to your brother or sister?
- What do you usually do on Saturday? Sunday?
- What time do you usually go to bed? Wake up?
- Are you more like your father or mother? (more similar to)
- How often do you exercise?
- Tell us a funny family story.
- Can you swim? Could you save someone?
- What does your mother do? Who cleans your room?
- When's your birthday?

Finished. ALREADY? Go the other way, and do the questions you skipped.

For example?

Say what? Really? Me too! Wow Awesome You're kidding No way That's too bad Bummer

Say what? Really? Me too! Wow Awesome You're kidding No way That's too bad Bummer Kind of Half and half

Where? When? Why? Who? How? How often? How long? What time? ***FOR EXAMPLE WHAT ABOUT YOU?***

keep going

What will you do next semester break?

Did you ever stay up all night studying? *Drinking?*

Do you study at home or in the library?

Who's more strict, your father or mother?

Tell us a joke.

① Sit in groups of 3.

If the question is in front of you, you ask it.

Who's your favorite male movie star? Female? Superhero?

that way

How long can you study without taking a break?

How many text messages do you send per day? Receive?

Have you ever been very sick or in the hospital?

Did you ever get a really bad haircut?

Are you good with computers?

Are you very talented at anything? Art, music, sports?

② Roll the dice. Or.

Do the yellow questions today, blue next class, and then purple. Or. Take turns asking any question.

How often do you clean your room? Make your bed?

Did you ever get home after sunrise? *How often?*

What about you?

How many times has your family moved?

Do you have a driver's license?

What's your dream job? What's your plan B?

Did anybody ever ask you out and you said "NO"?

What about you?

What does your father do? Exactly, what does he do?

Did you ever fall asleep and miss your subway stop?

What was your favorite subject last semester?

Do you like animals? Are you a dog person or a cat person?

Did you ever have a part-time job?

ROMANCE question!

Say what? Really? Me too! Wow Awesome You're kidding No way That's too bad Bummer Kind of Half and half

Where? When? Why? Who? How? How often? How long? What time? FOR EXAMPLE WHAT ABOUT YOU?

Kind of Half and half Where? When? Why? Who? How? How often? How long? What time?

1 Sports & Summer

Is this on your bucket list? *What is?*

Put a ✓ check, answer the questions, and come prepared to talk.

Sports Personality

1.	*Are you good at sports*	______	*or*	*the last one picked?*	______
2.	*Are you a joiner*	______	*or*	*a loner?*	______
3.	*Are you a fitness freak*	______	*or*	*a couch potato?*	______
4.	*Are you more of a sprinter*	______	*or*	*a distance runner?*	______
5.	*Are you an indoors person*	______	*or*	*an outdoors person?*	______
6.	*Do you prefer team sports*	______	*or*	*individual sports?*	______
7.	*Do you prefer the summer*	______	*or*	*winter Olympics?*	______

8. *What's your favorite sport to play?* ____________________ *To watch?* ____________________

9. *Who's your favorite sports star?* ____________________ *Team?* ____________________

10. *What's your favorite sport brand? (Nike, Reebok, Puma? etc)* ____________________

Why? For example? What about you?

Conversation Preparation

Are you good at sports? Can you swim? Ski? Snowboard?

Some shy people are actually quite aggressive.

GUY *Hi. My name's Jack.*

GAL *Hi, I'm Jackie! Neat. Nice to meet you.*

GUY *Same here. How was your summer vacation?*

GAL *The usual. I stayed home and watched a lot of TV. Basically I just **recharged my batteries**. **What about you?***

GUY *I went to the Philippines for a month to study English. It was an immersion program. We spoke only English.*

GAL *Like this class?*

GUY *Yeah. Say, you're pretty smart. And pretty.*

GAL *Why thank you. What's your major?*

GUY *Diplomacy.*

GAL *Ha. Too funny. That figures. Well, thanks anyway. How did you like the English program?*

GUY *Wait, what's your major?*

GAL *Sports Marketing. It's a new major.*

GUY *Cool. Anyway, the program was fine. We did English all morning and sports in the afternoon. Their philosophy is that eight hours a day is too long to focus on one thing.*

GAL *That's smart. Did you learn any sports, or get better at any?*

GUY *Well the good news is, **first**, I'm not fast, but I do have good **endurance**. I'm good at long distances. **Second**, I'm pretty **flexible** for a guy. I can almost do the splits. And **third**, I'm pretty **coordinated**. I never got very good at any one sport, but I did learn them pretty quickly.*

GAL *So, you're a **natural athlete**, but not an excellent athlete.*

GUY *Yeah, you could say that.*

GAL *Not to change the subject, but how were your grades last semester?*

GUY *No comment. Actually, I made B's in my **elective** courses and C's in my **major** courses.*

GAL *Maybe you should change your major?*

GUY *Yeah, I gave that a lot of thought. How were your grades?*

GAL *My **GPA** was 3.9. I'm OK with that. It was my first semester, and now I know how to **prioritize** my time. To **focus** on what's important.*

GUY *That's a good skill. I had a part-time job, and I think that hurt my grades. And of course skipping class didn't help.*

GAL *That's true. By the way, where's your textbook?*

GUY *Oh, I think that's another reason why my grades were so low.*

1. Listen & repeat
2. Listen & record
3. Listen to yourself

Several times

Write what you will say

Writing before Speaking improves Accuracy

Every question is about you, so you know all the answers.

1 **What did you do last summer?** *What did you do last weekend? What did you do last night?*
Last summer I was a ***couch potato****. All I did was sleep and watch TV. I did the dishes once.*

---

2 **What was your hardest class last semester?** *How many times did you take the Soonung test?*
My hardest class was Marketing. The professor lectured in English, and it was hard to follow.

---

3 **How many hours are you taking this semester?** *Did you drop any courses last semester?*
I'm taking 18 hours. Three major courses, four required courses, and two elective courses.

---

4 **Do you belong to a club?** *Is it a real club or just an excuse to meet and drink?*
I joined the guitar club. Luckily, they did not have an audition. My goal is to be in a band.

---

5 **Did you ever have a part-time job?** *Were you good at it? Were you ever fired?*
Last summer I tutored two students in math. And last semester I worked at 7-11.

---

6 **Are you good at sports? Any sport?** *What is your best and worst sport?*
I'm good at sports that require speed, like soccer. But bad at sports that require concentration, like golf.

---

7 **Are you talented at anything?** *Did you ever win a contest? Art, music, math, anything?*
I'm good at drawing and painting. My whole family is artistic, it runs in the family. My mother teaches art.

---

8 **Did you play any sports or learn any skills as a child?** *Taekwondo? Piano? Swimming?*
I took taekwondo for six years until high school. I was a third-degree black belt.

Really　Me too　Why?　When?　Where?　Who?　How often?
Anyway　Whatever　Kind of　Half and half　It depends

Talk about what you wrote

Speaking to many partners improves Fluency

Listen, read, and repeat the example answer, then write your own.

9 Can you swim? Can you ski? Snowboard? *Would you rather be an Olympic skier or swimmer?*
I took swimming lessons one summer when I was young. I can ski but I'm more into snowboards.

____

10 What was your best summer vacation? *What country or place is on your bucket list?*
My best vacation was last year. We took a road trip across the U.S., from LA to Florida. The Grand Canyon. Wow!

____

11 Do you come from a family of athletes or couch potatoes? *Is your father or mother into fitness?*
My family is pretty active. My father likes camping and hiking, and my mom belongs to a health club.

____

12 Did you ever go to a professional sports game? *What's your favorite sports team? Player?*
I went to a professional baseball game once. It was exciting for an hour, then I fell asleep.

____

13 Did you go to any theme parks or festivals last summer? *What's your favorite ride?*
We went to Caribbean Bay once, and that was awesome. And I also went to a girl group concert by the river.

____

14 Did you ever miss school because you were sick? *Were you ever injured playing a sport?*
Once my parachute didn't open while skydiving. Joke. I was in a minor car accident when I was seven.

____

15 Did you see any movies last summer? *Would you recommend it?*
I saw ***Avengers 17,*** *and I really liked it. I highly recommend it. For once, the story was relevant.*

____

16 What will you do after class? *What will you do this weekend?*
After class, I'll go to my guitar club meeting. Tomorrow we have a performance at the Musical Arts Center.

____

For example? What about you?

Vocabulary Buffet

Select words that help describe your life. If the meaning is not clear, look it up at: **dictionary.com**
Read the example sentences out loud. They pronounce the word for you. Listen and repeat. 10 times.
The world has changed. If you want to learn a new vocabulary, **YOU LEARN IT**. That's now **YOUR** job.

PERSONALITY OPPOSITES

always doing something	**active**	1	**couch potato**	*watches a lot of TV*
joins clubs, likes groups	**joiner**	2	**loner**	*likes being alone*
really, really likes fitness	**fitness freak, gym rat**	3	**lazy slob**	*a lazy and messy person*
likes indoor activities	**indoor person**	4	**outdoor person**	*likes outdoor activities*
is good at sports, but not smart	**jock**	5	**nerd, geek**	*very smart (computers) but not good at sports*
like a ballet dancer and figure skater	**graceful**	6	**awkward**	*runs like a duck, is a bad dancer also*
is productive in the morning	**morning person**	7	**evening person**	*is alert and productive in the evening*
runs fast, 100-meter race	**sprinter**	8	**distance runner**	*1000 meters to marathon*

9. **are into, buff** likes very much, very interested in. *My brother is into sports. My father is a history buff.*
10. **athletic** physical talent, good at sports. *My sister is athletic. She'd like to be a professional athlete.*
11. **athletic scholarship** free school for sport talent. *I got into here on an athletic scholarship, not brains.*
12. **black and blue** injured skin and muscle, turns blue. *I fell down the stairs and my leg is black and blue.*
13. **coach, referee, cheerleader** sport people *We lost the game but it was the referee.*
14. **concentration** totally focused on the subject. *Archery and fencing require concentration. And math.*
15. **endurance, stamina** can go a long time. *I have no endurance so I like speed skating and sprinting.*
16. **flexible, limber** can do the splits, like a ballerina. *My sister can do the splits. She's very flexible.*
17. **killer abs, six-pack** stomach muscles you can see. *Killer abs are on my bucket list.*
18. **last one picked** worst person in class at sports. *In elementary school I was always the last one picked.*
19. **muscular** has big muscles. *Those guys who work at the gym are very muscular.*
20. **natural athlete** good at sports with little practice. *He's a natural athletic, good at many sports.*
21. **no pain, no gain** no pain = no improvement. *It's not easy, there is no pill. No pain, no gain.*
22. **PE** physical education. I liked PE in high school. *I liked being outside and doing group things.*
23. **runs in the family** the whole family has the ability. *We all have musical talent. It runs in the family.*
24. **wannabe** wants to be good, but doesn't practice. *I'm just a wannabe. I don't have the dedication.*

SPORTS THAT REQUIRE:
concentration: archery, golf, billiards, bowling
quick reflexes: ping pong, basketball, fencing
coordination: diving, figure skating
speed: soccer, speed skating, track and field
endurance: marathon, swimming, iron man

GO	PLAY	TAKE / DO
bowling	badminton	aerobics
jogging	baseball	karate
skiing	basketball	Pilates
snowboarding	soccer	taekwondo
swimming	tennis	yoga

Vocabulary Buffet

PAIN TERMS (Ouch)

25. **ache, sore** slight to medium muscle pain. *My legs ache. My legs are sore.*
26. **blister** a little balloon on the skin from tight shoes. *My rollerblades gave me a blister.*
27. **faint / pass out** to lose consciousness. *She fainted. He passed out. (Women faint, men pass out.)*
28. **pulled muscle** muscle injury. *I started to spring full speed and pulled a muscle.*
29. **sprain** injured joint, like ankle or knee. *I sprained my ankle playing basketball. My ankle is sprained.*
30. **swollen** larger than normal, like a hurt ankle. *My ankle is swollen, and it hurts!*

University Opposites from Last Semester

very smart	**brainiac**	1	**slacker**	*lazy, unmotivated*
lenient	**easy grader**	2	**hard grader**	*strict*
an artist	**idea person**	2	**detail person**	*an accountant*
joins clubs	**joiner**	3	**loner**	*content when alone*
focused	**long attention span**	4	**short attention span**	*distracted*

UNIVERSITY TERMS

Years	Courses	Classes
freshmen	elective	2 hours
sophomore	required	3 hours
junior	minor	once a week
senior	major	twice a week

Learning teamwork

Learning black and blue

Vocabulary Check

This will improve your listening and vocabulary at the same time. Kill 2 birds with 1 stone. ***Cool.***

You will hear a short sentence with three possible answers, A, B, C. Mark the best answer with a big, black dot.

For example:

1. **A couch potato:**
   - **A** *Watches a lot of TV*
   - **B** *Likes vegetables*
   - **C** *Is in danger of pulling a muscle*

	1	2	3	4	5	6	7	8	9	10
A	●	○	○	○	○	○	○	○	○	○
B	○	○	○	○	○	○	○	○	○	○
C	○	○	○	○	○	○	○	○	○	○

Here's a great idea. Transcribe the test on MS Word, and then answer it. Do it with the book open and you can check your spelling. Time yourself. Gradually you'll get faster and better, and you can keep track of your progress. This will improve your listening, vocabulary, and typing in English. All are good skills to get a job.

Longer Answers with Details

Focus! Make good, long sentences, and try to use some new vocabulary.

1. Longer writing leads to longer, smoother and better speaking.
2. You've never said these things before, so read, record and listen to yourself. *Put some feeling into it.*

Example: What did you do last summer?

*Last summer I went to a computer academy and learned MS Word, Excel, and Powerpoint. I went there five days a week, from three to five o'clock. It was a one-month course, and the academy is near my house. My best friend went also and after class we would go hang out near the park and talk about what we learned. It was difficult but now I'm really **into** Powerpoint, and I'll take another course this winter vacation. It's too hard to do my homework and learn computer programs at the same time.*

1 **What did you do last summer?** ***Does your family go to the same place every summer?***

____

____

____

____

2 **Are you talented at anything?** ***Music, art, math, sports? What's your longest nap?***

____

____

____

3 **Where's your favorite place to hang out on the weekends?** ***What will you do this weekend?***

____

____

____

Last summer, did you take a road trip? Meet Mr. or Miss Right? Get in shape? (Extra points for all three)

Answer in Academic Format

This will improve your speaking, and your writing, in every language.

1. Academic means persuasive. You prove something with specific examples, ***first***, ***second***, ***third***.
2. For example: *My parents are strict, because of **1**, **2**, **3**. My parents are lenient. For example, **1**, **2**, **3**.*

1 Do you belong to a club? ***Why exactly? Why not?***

*Last week I joined the guitar club. I looked around for clubs and decided it was the best fit for me. **First**, I like music, and I'm already pretty good at piano. **Second**, I can kill two birds with one stone: I can learn a new instrument and make a new set of friends. **Third**, a really pretty girl in my Korean history class joined that club.*

____

____

____

____

2 Do you come from a family of athletes or couch potatoes?

*I definitely come from a family of fitness freaks. **First**, my parents are into fitness. They belong to a health club, and they often play in badminton tournaments. And my father coaches little league soccer. **Second**, my older sister is a ballet major and is very health-conscious. **Third**, I'm taking kick boxing and mixed martial arts.*

____

____

____

____

For example? What about you?

Pronunciation Practice

This audio takes only 3 minutes. In 10 minutes you could do it 3 times.

How do you get good at something? You do it more than once.

i	æ	ɛ	ɪ
bead	bad	bed	bid
beat	bat	bet	bit
cheap	chap	chep	chip
deed	dad	dead	did
eat	at	et	it

B	P	F	V
bail	pale	fail	veil
ban	pan	fan	van
bar	par	far	var
bare	pair	fare	vare
base	pace	face	vase

L	R	N	W
lack	rack	nack	wack
late	rate	Nate	wait
lay	ray	nay	way
lead	read	need	weed
leak	reek	neek	week

Say what?
You bet him or you bit him?

Descriptive Paragraph

1. Write your paragraph on computer, put your photo on it, and glue or staple it here.
2. Use some new vocabulary. You get points on your conversation test for new vocabulary.
3. Extra points if you include a photo. ***Double extra points if you are in the photo.***

It's important that you read and record this, and listen to yourself.
If you don't like the way you sound, how do you think your partners feel?

About Sports

I like sports because I'm good at them, and it gives me a kind of reputation. Also, I enjoy teaching others how to play sports, especially kids. It would be wonderful if I could be a professional ***athlete*** *of some kind, but if not, I think being a* ***coach*** *could be a good job. I used to be a* ***couch potato*** *and* ***indoor person****, but my father made me take* ***little league*** *baseball, and I found out that I was good at sports, and I like playing. I like the competition. Also, I'm a good* ***sprinter****, which helps in a lot of sports. My sports coach is a* ***fitness freak*** *and he's really* ***into sports****. Fitness is like a product he's trying to sell us. He's* ***muscular*** *and he has* ***killer abs****, but he's not a show off. Sports* ***runs in his family****, his brother and sister are also coaches. He runs the City* ***Marathon*** *every year, and he tries to get us to run the* ***half marathon****. He's very* ***limber****, and he used to be on the national gymnastics team. He went to an Olympics, but I forgot where. His particular interest is finding the best sport for each student, which one we are best in. However, I think he gave up on my best friend. Coach told him, "I think your best sport is jogging." Ha. Too funny.* (230 words)

TOEFL Essay

Answer a conversation question with a TOEFL essay.

1. Follow the example below and write your own TOEFL essay.
2. It has ABC in the introduction, ABC paragraphs with specific examples, and ABC in the conclusion.
3. Print two copies. Hand in one, and paste one here and use it for conversations in class.

You can see that the A B C are color-coded. *Neat.*

What you write about is what you're going to talk about in class, and on your conversation test.
So write about something that interests you! You can write about pretty much anything on the topic:

1. Your favorite sport, and three reasons why. Or, your three favorite sports.
2. Your hobby, and three reasons why. Or, your three favorite hobbies or interests.
3. The hobby of your whole family and three reasons why. Or, the top three hobbies.
4. The three reasons why you hate PE class.

A15 Amy Lawrence

Do you come from a family of athletes or couch potatoes?

My father is a ***fitness freak***, and we all take after him. Everyone in my family is the ***outdoor type***, and we are all good at sports. My parents are good at badminton, my brother is very good at taekwondo, and I am good at rollerblading. We are not experts, but we are good.

First, my parents' hobby is badminton, and they play every morning in a park near our house. They usually play doubles, and they are the champions in our apartment complex in Riverside. They have won several trophies in tournaments at our local health club. In addition, my father is a hapkido expert, and thee times a year he is a judge at hapkido tournaments.

Second, we are good at taekwondo. My older brother is a third degree black belt. He has been taking taekwondo since he was five years old. At first, he liked to do the poomsehs. But these days he likes to do high, spinning kicks. He has ***killer abs***. He is on the demonstration team at his dojang, and last year they performed at City Hall.

Third, we are good at rollerblading. I am the champion there! I have been rollerblading for three years. Lately I have been practicing going backwards. It took me a while to get the hang of it, but now I'm pretty good. I am also very fast and have great ***endurance***. I'm not good at jumping yet, but soon I will be. Soon I will try the skateboard, but first I need to buy a helmet.

Well, there it is. My whole family is in shape and good at sports. My parents are good at badminton, my brother at taekwondo, and I am good at rollerblading. We are not world champions, but we are all fit, healthy, and athletic. In sum, my father is super fit for a man his age, and he set the example for his whole family. (327)

1. Listen & repeat
2. Listen & record
3. Listen to yourself

Several times

Yes, it's homework,
but it's about YOU!
Get into it.

WRAP PARTY!

SPORTS

Are you active or a couch potato?
What's your favorite computer game?

Are you better at computer games or sports?
What's your favorite?

Are you a good dancer? Are you coordinated?
Are you graceful or awkward? Do you have rhythm?

Are you better at sports that require concentration, coordination, or speed?

Do you prefer the Olympics or the World Cup?
The summer or winter Olympics?

SUMMER

Did you travel last summer?
Have you ever travelled abroad?
Do you have a driver's license?

Did you ever go on a road trip? On a bike or on a train?
How many days?

Where did you hang out the most last summer?
Did you ever go to the library? Where did you play computer games?

Did you ever have a part-time job?
Did working hurt your grades? Do you get an allowance?

What's your hobby?
What's your favorite computer game? Is your family musically talented?

SEMESTER

Do you belong to a club? Are you a joiner or a loner?

What was your easiest course last semester? Your hardest course?

Do you use the weekends to rest, or catch up on your schoolwork?

If you could have free private lessons in any sport or skill, which would it be?

Did you play on any teams in high school?
Were you ever a team captain?

List your top 3 hobbies, talents, or interests

1. ______
2. ______
3. ______

High points of last summer

1. ______
2. ______
3. ______

Low points of last summer

1. ______
2. ______
3. ______

Use this to start conversations.

What's your . . .?

Really? No way Me too! • Kind of It depends Half and half • Where? When? Why? Who? How? How often? How long?

*First, second, third, finally • But, however, on the other hand • The bad news is • **FOR EXAMPLE? WHAT ABOUT YOU?***

Are you good at sports?

Listen, Repeat, Improve

SPORTS

What's your favorite sports team?
Who's your favorite player?
Did you ever see them in person?

Are you athletic?
How many sit-ups, push-ups and chin-ups can you do? Non-stop?
Are you a fast runner?

Are you an indoors person or an outdoors person?
Have you ever been camping?

Are you more of a jock or a nerd?
Were you ever the last one picked?

Are you better at sprints or long distances?
Did you ever win a foot race?

SPORTS

Did you exercise or play any sports last summer?
How often did you watch TV for six hours straight?

Do you prefer team sports or individual sports?
Why? For example?
Were you ever on a relay team?

If you could be world champion, which sport would it be in?
Where would you live?

Were you ever injured while exercising or playing a sport?
Did you break a bone or need stitches?

What's your favorite sports movie?
Moneyball? Jerry Maguire?

FAMILY

Did your father or a family member teach you any sports?
Were they patient?
Is your father a little league coach?

Are your parents into fitness and health?
Do they belong to a health club?

Is your neighborhood fitness friendly?
Is there a park, stream, or mountain nearby?

Does your father or mother work at home on the weekends?

Does your father have a hobby? What's your mother's hobby?
Do they like fishing, camping, skiing or hiking?

List your top 3:

Sports to play

1. __________
2. __________
3. __________

Sports you wish you could play

1. __________
2. __________
3. __________

Sports to watch

1. __________
2. __________
3. __________

Use this to start conversations.
What's your . . .?

Really? No way Me too! • Kind of It depends Half and half • Where? When? Why? Who? How? How often? How long?
First, second, third, finally • But, however, on the other hand • The bad news is • ***FOR EXAMPLE? WHAT ABOUT YOU?***

2 Tech & Texting

Geek, nerd, loner, indoors person, suspected hacker. Girl group wannabe.

Answer the questions and come prepared to talk. (Be an English nerd!)

Tech Personality

1. *Are you a nerd*	______	*or*	*more of a jock?*	______
2. *Are your parents tech savvy*	______	*or*	*ten years behind?*	______
3. *Are you an Apple person*	______	*or*	*a Windows person?*	______
4. *Do you prefer to talk*	______	*or*	*text?*	______
5. *Do you download legally*	______	*or*	*illegally?*	______
6. *Are you a bookworm*	______	*or*	*a slacker?*	______
7. *Are you a brainiac*	______	*or*	*a slow learner?*	______
8. *Are you an idea person*	______	*or*	*a detail person?*	______
9. *Are you an overachiever*	______	*or*	*an underachiever?*	______
10. *Do you prepare ahead of time*	______	*or*	*cram at the last minute?*	______

Why?

Really? No way! Wow. Me too. Where? When? Who? How?

Why? For example? What about you?

Conversation Preparation

Are you good with computers?

Listen, repeat, record.
Listen to yourself.
Several times.

GUY *Hi. My name's Jack.*

GAL *Hi, I'm Jackie! Nice to meet you.*

GUY *What did you do last weekend?*

GAL *Actually, I went computer shopping.*

GUY *No way. That's what I call taking your homework seriously. Did you buy one?*

GAL *Yeah. My father took me shopping, and he bought me an iMac desktop. The big one, 27 inch.*

GUY *Lucky you. Why not get something **portable**, like an Airbook or laptop?*

GAL *Well, **first**, I don't like to carry things around. My school books are heavy enough. **Second**, I really like having a big screen. It's great for watching movies and spotting mistakes when I do my homework. And **third**, my phone can do anything I need to do while traveling.*

GUY *I'm just the opposite. I love my **laptop**. It makes me very efficient, and I can work anywhere.*

GAL *Are you good with computers?*

GUY *I'm fairly good. My father is very **tech savvy**, and works for Samsung Electronics. He always has their newest models, and I get his used stuff.*

GAL *Lucky you. What **programs** do you know?*

GUY *I know the basics, **Word, Excel, Powerpoint**. I don't know a lot of programs, but the ones I know, I know well. And you?*

GAL *I know the basics like you, and I know some Adobe art programs, such as **Photoshop** and **InDesign**.*

GUY *Aha, that's why you like the big screen Mac. And I hear they are **user-friendly**.*

GAL *Exactly. Do you text a lot?*

GUY *Nah, **texting** is not my thing. I'd rather talk. I don't get texting. And you?*

GAL *I'm a **text-a-holic**. I text all the time. Hundreds every day.*

GUY *Wow. Who do you text?*

GAL *My mother, sister, classmates, boyfriend, everybody. And you?*

GUY *I'm an email guy. I just never got into texting. Spending my whole day typing just doesn't interest me. No offense.*

GAL *That's OK. I understand. The **bad news** about texting is that sometimes I get lost and send the wrong message to the wrong person.*

GUY *Yeah, I know. Last weekend you sent me a text. I guess you got my number off the class roll sheet.*

GAL *NO WAY!*

GUY *Just kidding.*

This is called 'multi-tasking' and 'prioritizing.'

Write what you will say

Writing before Speaking improves Accuracy

Ask ONE question. Talk a while. AFTER they answer, you can ask a red follow-up question.

1 What did you do last Saturday? *What did you do on Sunday? What did you do last winter?*
Last Saturday I slept late and then played computer games for 10 hours. I stopped when I got hungry.

___

2 Do you belong to Facebook? Twitter? Instagram? *Do you have your own website?*
I belong to Facebook. That's kind of the center of my social universe. I contact everyone from there.

___

3 What kind of phone do you have? *How much memory? How big is your data plan?*
I have an iPhone 12, the big one. Gold. It has 132GB. The data plan is unlimited. I surf a lot.

___

4 How many texts do you send and get per day? *What texting program do you use?*
I guess I do about average, about 100 texts out and in. I use Mini-many-chat. It's free and has great emojis.

___

5 Did you ever use your phone in an emergency?
I never did, but once my father saw a car accident, and he called the police and ambulance.

___

6 How many songs are on your phone? *Where do you get them from?*
I have about 200 songs, I get them from iTunes. Once a week I listen and transcribe a song.

___

7 What computer programs do you know? *Are you an expert at any?*
I know the basics: Word, Excel and Powerpoint. I want to learn Photoshop and Keynote.

___

8 Do you have a desktop computer and printer in your bedroom?
My older brother and I share a desktop computer. We have a printer. The text is clear but photos are so-so.

___

Really Me too Why? When? Where? Who? How often?
Anyway Whatever Kind of Half and half It depends

Talk about what you wrote

Speaking to many partners improves Fluency

Ask questions in order, or at random. Or even numbers today, odd numbers next class.

9 **Do you ever watch YouTube videos?** *How much time do you spend there per week?*
Oh, I love watching videos on YouTube. I like new movie clips and old music videos. For example, David Bowie.

10 **What's your favorite computer game?** *On a scale of 1 to 10, how good are you?*
I'm addicted to Starcraft. I play it every day for about an hour, and for hours on the weekends. I need help.

11 **What will be your next tech purchase?** *Do you prefer to shop online or on foot?*
I want to get some wireless earphones. I think those are so cool. I would also like a laptop, but a small one.

12 **Do you have any group chats on Kakao?** *Who all is in the group? How often do you chat?*
I have three groups, actually. My high school friends, my university friends, and my family.

13 **How many phones have you had in your life?** *How many have you lost? Broken?*
I've had about four phones. All hand-me-downs. Whenever my father gets a new phone, I get his old one.

14 **How often do you legally download a movie? Illegally?** *Would you recommend it?*
I never download, but my older brother downloads one English movie a week for his class. Legally, I think.

15 **Do you ever do any homework research online?** *Ever bought a ticket online?*
Sometimes I'll surf for articles for my Current Events class. I watched my mom get an airline ticket once.

16 **What will you do after school?** *What will you do this weekend?*
This weekend I'm going get a new phone. I lost mine last Friday night. My parents were not happy.

For example? What about you?

Vocabulary Buffet

Are you an idea person or a detail person? *Kind of, it depends, sometimes, half and half. For example?*

PERSONALITY OPPOSITES

bookworm studies a lot, their head in a book. *She's a bookworm. She's always studying.*
slacker lazy student, lazy worker. *He's a slacker. I told him to stop slacking off and focus.*

brainiac very smart. (brain + maniac). *My sister is a brainiac. She got a scholarship to Harvard.*
slow learner has a hard time learning. *In math, I'm a slow learner. It takes me forever to learn something.*

idea person has many ideas, a movie director. *She's an idea person, very creative. She writes short stories.*
detail person like an accountant, likes details. *He's a detail person. He can write computer code for hours.*

introvert a loner, can entertain themselves. *I'm an introvert. Big, noisy crowds make me nervous.*
extrovert outgoing, likes being around people. *He's an extrovert. He likes doing things with a lot of people.*

jock good at sports but not smart. *He's a jock. He's on the school soccer team.*
nerd, geek good with computers. *He's a nerd, a computer nerd. She's a science geek. Way smart.*

long attention span can study for a long time. *She has a long attention span. She can read a book, non-stop.*
short attention span needs a break every 20 minutes. *He has a short attention span. Ten minutes, tops.*

modern likes new technology, new thinking. *My father is modern, he's into modern technology.*
traditional, old fashioned likes the old ways. *My parents are old fashioned. My curfew is 9 p.m.*

procrastinate to delay, especially making a decision. *I procrastinate too much. I'm a procrastinator.*
prepare ahead of time, good to go to be prepared early. *Let's do it. I'm good to go.*

short fuse gets angry quickly. *When my father drives he has a short fuse. He's always blowing the horn.*
lot of patience is calm, never gets angry. *Our teacher has a lot of patience. Very laid back. Never gets angry.*

tech savvy good at, knows a lot about. *My brother is tech savvy. He knows code and makes websites.*
tech phobic, novice, newbie **phobic** means scared of. **Novice** and **newbie** mean beginners. *I'm a newbie.*

underachiever smart but gets low grades. *My parent's think I'm an underachiever, but I'm doing my best.*
overachiever not smart, but gets high grades. *I was an overachiever in high school. That wore me out.*

well-organized tidy, never loses things. *I'm well-organized. I get nervous when I am not prepared.*
scatterbrained disorganized and forgetful. *She's scatterbrained. Always losing things and forgetting stuff.*

FREQUENCY

How often do you?

Once, twice, three times a: day, week, month, year
5, 10, 20 times an hour. 100, 200 times a day
Every other: day, week, month, year
Once every two weeks, once every six months
very often, often, sometimes, it depends
rarely, seldom, every now and then, hardly ever
usually = normally = generally

COMPARISON

It was too	*Is more / less*
1. *complicated*	*affordable*
2. *expensive, cheap*	*comfortable*
3. *heavy, light*	*convenient*
4. *high-tech, old-fashioned*	*expensive*
5. *small, big / soft, hard*	*has . . . memory*
6. *thick, thin / tight, baggy*	*user-friendly*
7. *wide, narrow*	*quiet, noisy*

Vocabulary Buffet

PROGRAMS	SOCIAL PROGRAMS
Word, Excel	Facebook, Messenger
Powerpoint	Instagram
Photoshop	Pinterest
Illustrator	Skype, Snapchat
PDF	Twitter
Prezi	WhatsApp

SURFING SITES	FORMATTING TERMS
wikipedia.com	format
imdb.com	font / typeface
azlyrics.com	margins
Youtube	spacing
BBC.com	header
images.google.com	indent
translate.google.com	page size A4, 8.5 x 11

1. apps
2. blogs
3. Bluetooth
4. browser
5. CCTV
6. crash
7. cloud
8. flash drive
9. go viral
10. GPS
11. hacker
12. hot spot
13. icon
14. ID, password
15. intuitive
16. megapixel
17. memory stick
18. multi-tasking
19. navigation
20. netiquette
21. netizen
22. notebook, laptop
23. peer to peer
24. screen saver
25. search engine
26. selfie
27. snail mail
28. SNS
29. spam
30. USB
31. user friendly
32. video chat
33. voice recognition
34. Wi-Fi

The Swedish Texting Team

(I made that up.)

Enter what? Where?

Vocabulary Check

This will improve your listening and vocabulary at the same time. Kill 2 birds with 1 stone. *Cool.*

You will hear a short sentence with three possible answers, A, B, C. Mark the best answer with a big, black dot.

For example:

1. A slacker is a:

A *Lazy overachiever*

B *Diligent overachiever*

C *Lazy underachiever*

	1	2	3	4	5	6	7	8	9	10
A	O	O	O	O	O	O	O	O	O	O
B	O	O	O	O	O	O	O	O	O	O
C	●	O	O	O	O	O	O	O	O	O

Longer Answers with Details

Focus! Make good, long sentences, and try to use some new vocabulary.

1. Longer writing leads to longer, smoother and better speaking.
2. You've never said these things before, so read, record and listen to yourself. *Put some feeling into it.*

Example: What's your favorite computer game? *Are you addicted?*

My favorite game is **World of Warcraft.** *I play every day after school before I go to my academy. The PC room is on my way to the academy, so that's convenient. It's actually cheaper to play in a computer room, and I like the competitive atmosphere. There's a kind of energy from all the players. I know it's a waste of time, but it's kind of recess for my mind. It helps keep me from getting burned out at school.*

1 What's your favorite computer game? *App? Tech brand? Mobile game? Shopping site?*

____

____

____

2 What computer programs do you know? *Did you ever go to a computer academy?*

____

____

____

3 Do you ever go to YouTube? *What do you watch? What's your favorite video?*

____

____

____

How many? How much? How often? How long? How many times?

Nerd wannabe

Answer in Academic Format

This can also be the start of your TOEFL Essay. Kill 2 birds with 1 stone.

1. Academic means persuasive. You prove something with specific examples, ***first***, ***second***, ***third***.
2. For example: *My parents are strict, because of **1**, **2**, **3**. My parents are lenient. For example, **1**, **2**, **3**.*

1. Is your family high-tech? ***Do you live in one of those new high tech apartments?***

Half and half. *My father and I are **techies**. My father is very tech savvy. He has the latest technology on his computers and in his cars. If I ask for something tech, he'll get it, no questions asked. **On the other hand**, my mother and sister are like, whatever. My mother shops online, and my sister sends about a million texts a day.*

____

____

____

____

2. What's your most important tech device? Or. What are your three most important tech devices?

*My most important piece of tech is my laptop. I use it for everything. **First**, I use it instead of my phone for text messages. I like the bigger keyboard and screen. **Second**, I use it for entertainment and to watch movies and surf the internet. **Third**, I use it for education, meaning I can do my homework on it.*

____

____

____

____

For example? What about you?

Pronunciation Practice

All human learning can be summed up in three words: *Watch, try, repeat.* This activity is very repetitive. *Got it?*

i	æ	ɛ	ɪ
feed	fad	fed	fid
feet	fat	fet	fit
he'd	had	head	hid
heat	hat	het	hit
lead	lad	led	lid
lease	lass	less	liss

B	P	F	V
bat	pat	fat	vat
bed	ped	fed	ved
beel	peel	feel	veal
beer	peer	fear	veer
berry	Perry	ferry	very
bet	pet	fet	vet

L	R	N	W
led	red	Ned	wed
leel	real	kneel	wheel
leer	near	rear	we're
len	ren	nen	when
life	rife	knife	wife
light	right	night	white

Th	T	D
thin	tin	din
theme	team	deem
there	tear	dare
therm	term	derm
think	tink	dink
this	tis	dis

Descriptive Paragraph

1. Write your paragraph on computer, put your photo on it, and glue or staple it here.
2. Use some new vocabulary. You get points on your conversation test for new vocabulary.
3. Extra points if you include a photo. ***Double extra points if you are in the photo.***

It's important that you read and record this, and listen to yourself.
If you don't like the way you sound, how do you think your partners feel?

Something about technology

*I love modern technology. I can't imagine the world before cell phones. That's like, the age of dinosaurs or something. Can you imagine writing something on paper by hand? How would you **cut and paste** and move paragraphs around? No way. The computer programs I know are **Word** and **Excel**. That's all I know but I know them pretty well. I use them on my **desktop** (it has a 27 inch screen) and **laptop** (13 inch screen). Every Sunday night I play a popular English song (usually a ballad) on my computer several times and try to transcribe it. Then I go to **azlyrics.com** or **lyrics.com** and check to see if I got the **lyrics** right. I also go to **imdb.com** (International Movie Data Base) and **surf** around. That site is **user-friendly.** The **icons** are very **intuitive**, and the **search engine** is very good. And anytime I want to know anything I go to **Wikipedia.com**. Those are my three main sites. For social sites I use **Facebook** messenger and **Snapchat**. On my cell phone I love the maps and GPS function. They're so neat. From my laptop and phone I **backup** everything on the **cloud,** and then store it on my desktop. I have a **paranoia** about losing something, so I **backup** all the time. My father uses **Google**, especially **Google Drive** and **Google Docs**. He uses them a lot for work, and he's showing me. Finally, I'm trying to get the hang of using the **voice recognition** on my phone. It's helping me to improve my English.*

Answer any conversation question from the unit with a TOEFL essay.

1. Follow the example below and write your own TOEFL essay.
2. It has ABC in the introduction, ABC paragraphs with specific examples, and ABC in the conclusion.

You can see that the A B C are color-coded. *Neat.*

What you write about is what you're going to talk about in class, and on your conversation test.
So write something that interests you! You can write about pretty much anything on the topic:

1. Your favorite tech device and three reasons why. Or, your three favorite tech devices.
2. Your favorite app and three reasons why. Or, your three favorite apps.
3. Your favorite program, or your three favorite programs.
4. Three ways technology helps you with your education.

A15 Amy Lawrence

What's your favorite tech device?

I just could not live without my iPhone. I use it every day in many ways. In fact, I probably use it way too much. If I studied as much as I used my phone, I could probably get a ***scholarship*** and pay my parents back for the phone. Anyway. Mainly I use my phone for entertainment, education and communication.

First, I use my phone for entertainment. I ***commute*** to school every day for a total of two hours, so I have a lot of ***time to kill***. While on the subway I watch my favorite TV shows, mainly *Descendents of the Sun*. Song Hye-kyo is a little old for Song Joon-ki, but that's OK. I have watched every ***episode*** at least four times. I also surf the internet for TV star ***gossip***, and I get my daily news in English from the internet, usually the Korea Herald. I have about 400 selfies.

Second, my phone is great for education. Whenever a person or place is mentioned in a movie or on the news I look it up on Wikipedia.com. For example, last week there was a ***documentary*** on General MacArthur, and so I researched him on Wikipedia. I wanted to see an ***impartial*** opinion of him, written recently. Therefore, I looked at two articles, one that liked him and one that did not.

Finally, I use my phone for communication. Really. My boyfriend and I text about 200 times a day. Actually, I heard he used to text his old girlfriend 300 times a day, so I am a little jealous. On the other hand, we don't actually communicate, we just send little ***emoticons*** back and forth. I live in a ***boarding house*** near school so every morning and night my mother calls to check up on me.

Well, like everything else, the phones these days are ***good-news, bad-news***. The good news is that the phones are very useful. I use my phone for entertainment, education and communication. And of course I take a ton of photos. The bad news is that my phone is also a ***black hole*** of lost time. I spend hours and hours texting and surfing and have nothing to show for it. In sum, the iPhone is expensive, and I waste a lot of time on it. The great news is that for something so small, it is very powerful, and ultimately it changes my life for the better. (423 words)

Listen, repeat, record.
Listen to yourself.
Just do it.

Yes, it's homework,
but it's about YOU!
Get into it.

WRAP PARTY!

PERSONALITY	TECH	TECH	SCHOOL
Are you an idea person or a detail person? *For example?*	**Do you belong to Facebook?** *How much time do you spend there every week?*	**Do you spend a lot of time on Youtube?** *For example?*	**How often do you get something printed at school at the**
Are you a bookworm or a slacker? *For example?*	**Who's best at technology in your family?**	**Can you listen to music when you do your homework?**	**Who's your most hi-tech teacher?** *Who's the lowest tech?*
Are you more of a jock or a nerd? *For example?*	**What online shopping mall do you use?** *Do you buy books? Clothes?*	**Did you ever show someone how to use a phone or computer?**	**Did you ever stay up all night studying?** *What was the result?*
Are you well-organized or do you often lose things? *For example?*	**How many phones have you had in your life?**	**What's your password?** **Just kidding.**	**How long can you study without taking a break?**
Do you like team projects? Are you a joiner	**Did your computer ever crash because of a virus?**	**What phone app do you use the most?**	**How many hours a week do you study?** *Where do you study?*

What's your?

1. ____________ most important class?
2. ____________ easiest class?
3. ____________ hardest class?
4. ____________ most interesting class?
5. ____________ most boring class?
6. ____________ biggest class? (most students)
7. ____________ smallest class?
8. ____________ longest class?
9. ____________ earliest class?

Ask the first question, talk about it for a while, then ask the next question.

Why exactly?

Really? No way Me too! • Kind of It depends Half and half • Where? When? Why? Who? How? How often? How long?

First, second, third, finally • But, however, on the other hand • The bad news is • ***FOR EXAMPLE? WHAT ABOUT YOU?***

Are you good with computers?

PERSONALITY	TECH	TECH	SCHOOL
Do you have a long or short attention span? *For example?*	What kind of computer do you have? *How old is it?*	Did you ever drunk-dial someone? *Did you ever send a text or email and then regret it?*	Did you ever get a low grade because you were not good with a certain program?
Are you a brainiac or a slow learner? *For example?*	Can you use Powerpoint? *Can you make a website?*	Did your parents ever punish you by taking away your phone?	Do any of your classes use technology for attendance?
Do you prepare ahead of time or cram at the last minute? *For example?*	What search engine do you usually use?	How many friends do you text on a regular basis?	Do you think our school's website is user-friendly? *For example?*
Are you an underachiever or overachiever?	How many selfies are on your phone? Do you use Snapchat?	How many songs are on your phone? *What kind, mainly?*	Do you ever use the computer lab at school? *Which building?*
When you have a tech problem, do you get the manual or start pushing buttons?	Do you prefer shopping online or on foot? *Where? Which site?*	What was your last tech purchase? *What's your next tech purchase?*	What do you think is rude phone behavior? *How often do you do that?*

List your top 3 apps

1. ______
2. ______
3. ______

What programs are you best at?

1. ______
2. ______
3. ______

What websites do you visit the most?

1. ______
2. ______
3. ______

Use this to start conversations.

What's your . . .?

Really? No way Me too! • Kind of It depends Half and half • Where? When? Why? Who? How? How often? How long?

First, second, third, finally • But, however, on the other hand • The bad news is • ***FOR EXAMPLE? WHAT ABOUT YOU?***

3 Romance & Finance

Romantic & Working Personality

1. *Do you believe in love at first sight* ______ *or true love takes time?* ______
2. *Do you forgive and forget* ______ *or hold a grudge?* ______
3. *Do you want a femme fatale* ______ *or a girl next door type?* ______

   Do you prefer the macho type ______, *a bad boy* ______, *or a nice guy?* ______
4. *Are you the faithful type* ______ *or a playboy / playgirl?* ______
5. *Are you a material girl / guy* ______ *or spiritual?* ______
6. *Are you trusting* ______ *or the jealous type?* ______
7. *Is your mother / father an idea person* ______ *or a detail person* ______
8. *Is your mother / father a workaholic* ______ *or a slacker?* ______
9. *Is your mother / father a lone wolf* ______ *or a team player?* ______
10. *Is your mother / father a company man* ______ *or an entrepreneur?* ______

Why? For example? What about you?

Conversation Preparation

Do you believe in love at first sight?

Oh, that's cold.

GUY *Hi. My name's Jack.*

GAL *Hi, I'm Amy. We met, I think, two weeks ago.*

GUY *Oh yeah. Sorry. I remember now. You were, kind of, I don't know, unhappy that day.*

GAL *Really? I'm usually a* ***happy camper****. Oh wait, I remember now. I* ***broke up with*** *my boyfriend two weeks ago. That must have been it.*

GUY *Bummer. I hear that love hurts.*

GAL *Well, not any more. He's history.*

GUY *If it's not too personal, why did you break up?*

GAL *Well* ***first****, he was all hands. Too* ***touchy-feely****. It was like dating an octopus.* ***Second****, he was* ***cheap****, he wanted to go halves all the time. And* ***third****, I caught him* ***cheating on*** *me.*

GUY *Sorry that I asked.*

GAL *Oh, that's OK. I'm over him. My mom says: "For pretty girls, men are like buses: another one will be along in 15 minutes."*

GUY *Ha. Too true.*

GAL *What about you? Do you have a girlfriend?*

GUY *No, I've got no time and no money, and no interest from any girl. And I don't like to chase. My mom says: "Good things come to those who wait."*

GAL *Ha. What does your dad say?*

GUY *He says I should get a part-time job: "No finance, no romance." Say, maybe your ex-boyfriend should talk to my dad.*

Listen, repeat, record.
Listen to yourself.

GAL *Tell me about it. Anyway. How did your parents meet?*

GUY *My father's a doctor, and my mother's a nurse. The usual story. I'm sure you've seen it on TV.*

GAL *Got it. How long did they date? Was it* ***love at first sight****?*

GUY *It was for my mom, but they dated for four years. She heard that my dad chased every pretty new nurse, and she wanted to be certain of his, uh, goals. She* ***played hard to get****. For a long time.*

GAL *Smart mom. Does your mom still work?*

GUY *Yes, she loves her job.* ***First****, my father is on call 24/7, but she works just 9 to 5 weekdays. No overtime, no weekends. And* ***second****, the hospital is across the street from our house. Very convenient.*

GAL *About my ex boyfriend. I thought being a* ***campus couple*** *would be convenient. But the bad news is, after you break up, you see them every day. Ugh. Anyway, my mom says that was only* ***puppy love****.*

GUY *Well, my father warned me about pretty girls. He said: "The prettier the rose, the sharper the thorns."*

GAL *Ouch.*

Write what you will say

Writing before Speaking improves Accuracy

This is writing practice. ***PUT SOME EFFORT INTO IT.***

1 **What did you do last weekend?**
I worked at my part-time job at GS25. I worked from midnight to 8:00 a.m. and slept all day Sunday.

____

2 **Do you have a boy / girlfriend?** *Do you wish you had one? Two? (joke)*
I have a girlfriend, but if you ask her, she'll say that "He's just a friend." I hate that.

____

3 **What's most important to you in a boy or girlfriend: looks, money, height, face, or body?**
Definitely looks and height. I have enough personality for two, so that's not a problem.

____

4 **Do you believe in love at first sight?** *Well then, how long does it take?*
I used to, but nobody has ever fallen in love with me at first sight. That's obviously not my fault.

____

5 **Did you ever have a crush on someone?** *Admired someone from afar?*
I had a crush on my middle school math tutor. Then, I saw his girlfriend and realized I had no chance.

____

6 **Did a boy or girl ever try to talk to you, or ask you out, and you said "No." ?**
Yes! A boy started talking to me in Starbucks, and I got so flustered I left without waiting for my coffee.

____

7 **Would you ever date a foreigner?** *Would your parents let you? Your grandparents?*
I would date a foreigner. That would be OK. But, marriage is a whole other ball game.

____

8 **What's your type?** *Who's your favorite opposite sex movie star? Do you have a celebrity crush?*
I like baby-face beautiful, like Jennifer Lawrence and Scarlett Johannson. My favorite actress is Emma Stone.

____

Really   Me too   Why?   When?   Where?   Who?   How often?   How long?
Awesome   Bummer   Anyway   Whatever   Kind of   It depends

Talk about what you wrote

Speaking to many partners improves Fluency

Make good, long sentences and try to use some new vocabulary.

9 **What's your dream job?** *What's your plan B?*
My dream job is to own my own advertising agency. Plan B is to work freelance until I can start my own company.

---

10 **What does your father do? What does your mother do?** *Do they like their jobs?*
My father is a high school math teacher, and my mother is a pharmacist. They're both workaholics.

---

11 **Is your father, mother, a workaholic?** *A slacker? A lone wolf or a team player? A suit?*
They are both workaholics. My mother is a suit at Samsung, and my father is a self-employed accountant.

---

12 **How did your parents meet?** *How long did they date? What is their age gap?*
My parents were a campus couple. They dated for four years, and their age gap is two years. Mom is older.

---

13 **What did your parents tell you about the opposite sex?** *What time is your curfew?*
My mom said that men are wolves, and I should be careful around them. My curfew is 8 p.m. every night.

---

14 **Do you have any opposite sex friends who might, maybe, someday be your boy / girlfriend?**
Well, there is one girl who is a possibility. I'm not sure if she's out of my league or not.

---

15 **How many people of the opposite sex do you text with?** *How is their grammar?*
I text with a few girls in my major, but they are not my type, and they have boyfriends, so, that leads nowhere.

---

16 **What will you do this weekend?** *What will you do after class? What will you do on Saturday?*
This weekend we'll have a practice date meeting with guys in this class. Next week, guys from another school.

For example? What about you?

Dating Buffet

ROMANTIC OPPOSITES

shows physical attention	**affectionate, touchy-feely**	1	**cold fish, cold**	*does not like being touched*
faithful	**faithful**	2	**playgirl/playboy**	*has several boy/girlfriends*
to forgive someone quickly	**forgive and forget**	3	**hold a grudge**	*stay mad at for a long time*
average girl	**girl next door type**	4	**femme fatale**	*French, meaning sexy girl*
needs a lot of attention	**high maintenance**	5	**low maintenance**	*easy to keep happy*
to keep secret information	**keep a secret**	6	**gossip, blabbermouth**	*talks about scandal stories*
to pretend to like someone	**lead somebody on**	7	**be led on**	*to believe, wrongly, that someone likes you*
thinks and acts modern	**modern**	8	**traditional, old-fashioned**	*likes the old ways*
humble, gives credit to others	**modest**	9	**stuck-up, vain**	*has a very high opinion of themselves*
very trustful	**trusting**	10	**jealous**	*Do not give attention to anyone but me!*

11. **admired from afar** you have a high opinion of them but were too shy to tell them. *I admired her from afar.*
12. **blind date** a date with a stranger. *I had a blind date last weekend. I've had two blind dates in my life.*
13. **campus couple** a couple who go to the same school. *My parents were a campus couple.*
14. **cheap date** a guy who spends only a little money on the date. *He's a cheap date. He's history.*
15. **chemistry** to have mental attraction. *We had good chemistry on the blind date.*
16. **crushed, have a crush on** **CRUSHED** = very sad, **HAVE A CRUSH ON** = to like someone very much. *I was crushed when I saw her kiss that guy. I had a crush on her all through middle school.*
17. **dating around** to date several people, one after another. *Date around before you go steady.*
18. **Dear John letter** a letter to end the relationship. *I got a Dear John letter when I was in the army.*
19. **fix up, play cupid** to arrange a date *Can you fix me up with your friend? I fixed her up with my cousin.*
20. **go steady** to date someone for more than six months. *They're going steady. They went steady for a year.*
21. **love at first sight** to love someone at first sight. *It was love at first sight. They fell in love at first sight.*
22. **love triangle** two men and one woman, or two women and one man. *Like in Titanic. It was a love triangle.*
23. **Mr. Right / Miss Right** the one who is right for you. *He's Mr. Right. I'm still searching for Miss Right.*
24. **out of your league** someone who is too good for you. *You're a nice guy, but she's out your league.*
25. **picky** hard to please *She's too picky. She finds something wrong with every guy.*
26. **platonic friend, just a friend** you like them, but not romantically. *He's a platonic friend. He's just a friend.*
27. **playing hard to get** to pretend you're not interested, to make them want you more. *I'm playing hard to get. I played hard to get. I played too hard to get, and he gave up.*
28. **puppy love** intense first love. *She's in puppy love. It's puppy love, you'll forget him next week.*
29. **secret admirer** you like someone and leave an anonymous note. *Ah! You have a secret admirer.*
30. **stood up, stand up** to break a promise and not show up. *I got stood up. She stood me up.*
31. **tease** to make a dog jump up, but never give him the cookie. *Be careful, she's a tease. She's teasing you.*
32. **the silent treatment** to not talk to someone you are mad at. *She gave me the silent treatment.*
33. **unrequited love** one-sided love, love that is unreturned. *It was a case of unrequited love. Bummer.*
34. **whirlwind romance** a very fast romance. *It was a whirlwind romance. They dated for only two months.*

Job Buffet

WORKING OPPOSITES

Meaning	Term	#	Term	Meaning
a bad, mean boss	**boss from hell**	1	**pushover**	*kind, very lenient*
hard work, training, to be boss someday	**career track**	2	**mommy track**	*doesn't work late or on weekends*
faithful worker, will never leave	**company man**	3	**entrepreneur**	*opens new businesses*
creative, has ideas, like a movie director	**idea person**	4	**detail person**	*like an accountant or programmer*
prefers to work alone	**lone wolf**	5	**team player**	*works well with others*
friendly, outgoing, good salesperson	**people person**	6	**anti-social**	*wants to be left alone, not friendly*
action figure, doesn't wait for orders	**self-starter**	7	**watch the clock**	*very anxious for work to end*
loves their work and works a lot	**workaholic**	8	**slacker**	*lazy worker*

WORKPLACE TERMS

1. **freelance** works for several people, like a freelance photographer or web designer. *She works freelance.*
2. **intern** an unpaid worker who takes the job to get the experience, and maybe get hired later.
3. **self-employed** has their own small business, a self-employed architect, taxi driver, photographer.
4. **suit** someone in power, wears a suit, an executive. *My father's a suit, but I'm not sure exactly what he does.*
5. **worker bee** a regular worker. *He's a worker bee. Just a normal worker, comes home tired every night.*

Chemistry nerds campus couple. So cute.

Suits. And, ex campus couple.

Vocabulary Check

This will improve your listening and vocabulary at the same time. Kill 2 birds with 1 stone. Cool.

You will hear a short sentence with three possible answers, A, B, C. Mark the best answer with a big, black dot.

	1	2	3	4	5	6	7	8	9	10
A	O	O	O	O	O	O	O	O	O	O
B	O	O	O	O	O	O	O	O	O	O
C	O	O	O	O	O	O	O	O	O	O

1 Take the quiz
2 Transcribe it
3 Check your answers

Longer Answers with Details

Focus! Make good, long sentences, and try to use some new vocabulary.

1. Longer writing is longer, smoother and better speaking.
2. You've never said these things before, so read, record and listen to yourself. *Put some feeling into it.*

1 **What's your parent's love story?** ***(Boy meets girl. . .?) How, how long, where?***

2 **What does your father do?** ***Exactly what? Where's his office? How long has he worked there?***

3 **What does your mother do?** ***Exactly what? Where's her office? How long has she worked there?***

4 **Tell me about your first crush.** ***A nurse, tutor, study partner, librarian, cheerleader, cute cashier?***

The secret to success in life is **sincerity**. When you can fake that, you've got it made.

Answer in Academic Format

This will improve your speaking, essays, and presentations.

Give specific names, places, emotions.

1. **Will you ever marry?** ***Why? Why not? Do you want kids? Are you scared of being old and lonely?***

   *I definitely want to marry, but first I need three things: **First**, I need money. A good job. **Second**, I would like to have a nice home or apartment before I marry. In short, I want to be financially stable first. **Third**, I need the perfect woman. A partner, a soul mate. My father says marriage should be a conversation, not a negotiation. My mother says love is a mirror. You can only take the amount of love you make.*

   ____

   ____

   ____

   ____

2. **What are the top qualities of a good boyfriend / girlfriend?**

   ***First**, I like someone who is funny, who can make me laugh. A sense of humor. I hate boring people. **Second**, I hate guys who are cheap. They have to pay. I know this is not gender equality, but I don't care. **Third**, I have to be number one. If he would rather hang out with his male friends, he can find another girlfriend. **Finally**, I like tall and athletic. Muscles. Face is not that important, but height and body are.*

   ____

   ____

   ____

   ____

For example? What about you?

Pronunciation Practice

Listen to yourself. *Are you getting better?* Why don't you do this in front of a mirror? Or video yourself?

i	æ	ɛ	ɪ
neat	nat	net	knit
peet	pat	pet	pit
reed	rad	red	rid
deed	dad	dead	did
eat	at	et	it
he'd	had	head	hid

B	P	F	V
bew	pew	few	view
bile	pile	file	vile
bine	pine	fine	vine
bun	pun	fun	vun
by	pie	phi	vie
bast	past	fast	vast

G, J	Ch	Z	Sh	S
gin	chin	zen	shin	sin
gyp	chip	zip	ship	sip
Jack	chak	Zak	shack	sack
Jane	chain	Zane	Shane	sane
jew	chew	zoo	shoe	Sue
Joe	cho	Zoh	show	so

Descriptive Paragraph

1. Write your paragraph on computer, put your photo on it, and glue or staple it here.
2. Answer any question in the unit. Answer in detail, something you want to talk about.
3. **EXTRA POINTS if you include a photo. Double extra points if you are in the photo.**

Write something about Dating, Romance, Rejection or Friendship

(If you like, you can write about your parents' courtship.)

*My **Mr. Right** will be tall and good-looking, but not too good looking. I don't like people who are **vain**. And if my boyfriend is really handsome, too many girls will **flirt** with him. A very good-looking mate can be **high maintenance**. I'd like somebody who is **affectionate**, but not affectionate in public. But I also don't want a **cold fish** either. Of course, my **ideal man** must be **faithful**. And he must **trust** me. I do not like **jealous** or **possessive** boyfriends.*

*I believe in **love at first sight**, because my father says that's what happened to him. He saw my mom in a restaurant near work and thought: I'm going to marry her. Mom says that story is not true, but dad swears it is. But they did have a **whirlwind romance**, they dated for only six months before getting married. Mom said she tried to **play hard to get**, but dad was just too cute. And funny. Her mom told her when she was a teenager: find guys who make you laugh, and marry the best-looking one. My father says that, A) he IS good-looking, but B) mom is **superficial**. Of course, mom was out of town when he told me that.*

Answer a conversation question with a TOEFL essay.

Follow the example and write your own. ***Write something that interests you!***

You can see that the A B C are color-coded. *Neat.*

I suggest you write about your Mr. or Miss Right. What qualities are most important to you? Character? Personality? Money? Looks? Face? Body? Height? Family? Intelligence? Sense of humor?

You could write about the three most important qualities of a good parent, father, mother, teacher or professor. Be specific with your specific examples.

A15 Amy Lawrence

Describe your Mr. Right / Miss Right

My parents advised me to play the field and date around a while before ***going steady***. They said I should not go steady with the first boy I meet. Actually, I dated a boy in high school, but my parents never found out. It was only ***puppy love***, but for two whole weeks I was in heaven! From that boy, Mr. X, I learned what qualities I want in ***Mr. Right***: I want looks, money, and body.

First, I am not the ***superficial*** type, but I would like my husband to be good looking. First, I want good-looking kids, and for that I need a good-looking husband. Second, there is ***prestige*** to having a handsome man. The bad news is, some good-looking men are not ***faithful***. My father is good-looking and ***faithful***, and my mother told me how she trained him. (And, she has a 4th degree black belt in taekwondo.)

Second, I am not a ***material girl***, but I would like financial security for my family. I would like a nice new apartment, nice car, and European vacations. I will work to help, but I want my kids to have the advantage of good schools and a good education. I do not want to worry about money my whole life, so I would never date a poor man. I did that in high school. Never again. Show me the money!

Third, I want my husband to be tall and well-built, because I want my kids to be tall and healthy. I do not want someone who is overweight, because I am a little overweight. If I marry someone like that, our kids will have to diet their whole life. No way do I want that. Studies show that tall people make more money and get more promotions.

Finally, I think most people will pick personality, but I think that's wrong. Everybody is nice to people they like, so if they like you, of course, you will like their personality. Children don't come from personality, they come from physical attraction. Anyway, I want my children to be good-looking, have enough money to have a good life, and to be tall and healthy. (366 words)

ABC	Specific examples
A: Looks	Prestige to having a good looking husband
B: Money	Nice apartment, car, vacations
C: Body	Tall and healthy

Did you ever notice that a lot of couples look alike?

Here's why. Everybody thinks they are attractive, so, anybody who looks like them is also attractive.

Just do it.

You can record audio and video! *Get into it.*

Hey! Go back and listen to your first recording.

You can hear your progress.

WRAP PARTY!

PERSONALITY

Do you have a boyfriend / girlfriend?
Are they in this class? Do they go to this school?

Would you rather be taller, better looking, smarter, or better at English?

Can you keep a secret, or, are you a gossip or tattletale?

Which one of your friends is the biggest moocher?
Can I borrow your pen? Joke

Did you ever get a Dear John letter? Text? Email?
Did you ever send one?

ROMANCE

Do you secretly like your best friend's girlfriend / boyfriend?

Which movie star would you like your boy / girlfriend to look like?

Girls: would you ever date someone younger than you?
Guys, older than you?

Is it fair that only guys have to go in the military?
What kind of service could females do?

Do you secretly admire anyone these days?
Did you ever have a crush on a teacher or a tutor?

PARENTS

What does your father do? What does your mother do?

How did your parents meet?
What's their age gap? How old were they when they got married?

Are your parents romantic?
Do they ever have a date night? What do they do on their anniversary?

Do your parents ever work at home?
Do they ever work on the weekends?

Do your parents like your friends?
Where do you hang out more: your house or their house?

FINANCE

Did you ever have a part-time job?
Ever have a work place romance?

Would you rather have a high-paying, stressful job or a fun, low-paying job?

Is your father / mother an idea person or a detail person?
A lone wolf or a team player?

Is your father / mother a workaholic or a slacker?
A people person or an introvert?

Is your father / mother a life-long, loyal company worker or an entrepreneur?

Who are the 3 most beautiful females on the planet?

1. ____________
2. ____________
3. ____________

Who are the 3 best-looking males?

1. ____________
2. ____________
3. ____________

Are you attracted to a certain type?

____

What are the top 3 jobs you would like to have?

1. ____________
2. ____________
3. ____________

For example? Why exactly? When? Who? How? How long? What about you?

Do you believe in love at first sight?

PERSONALITY	ROMANCE	PARENTS	FINANCE
Do you believe in love at first sight? *Well, how long does it take?*	**Are you a good liar?** *What's the biggest lie you ever told? What's the biggest lie you ever told your parents?*	**Do you belong to a club just to hang out with the opposite sex?** *For example?*	**Does your father / mother like their job?** *How long have they had it?*
Do you forgive and forget or hold a grudge? *Are you mad at anyone now?*	**Are you nervous around the opposite sex?** *Are you nervous around really good-looking members of the opposite sex?*	**Is your family affectionate?** *Does everybody touch and hug at family gatherings?*	**Does your father or mother ask if you need some money before you go out on Saturday night?**
Did somebody ever lead you on? *To copy your homework? Did you ever lead anybody on?*	**Is your mother the femme fatale type or the girl next door type?**	**What time is your curfew?** *What is the latest you ever got home?*	**Is your father / mother modern or old fashioned?** *Strict or lenient? Generous on your birthday?*
Did someone ever ask you out for coffee or something, and you said 'No'?	**Have you ever been stood up?** *How long did you wait? Did you ever stand anybody up?*	**What's the worst you were ever punished?** *What did you do? What did your parent's do?*	**What quality do you like best about the opposite sex?** *What do you dislike?*
Do you think co-ed schools are better? *Why? For example?*	**Would you rather hang out with one or two friends, or a bunch of people?**	**Is it fun to hang out with the opposite sex, or is it too much trouble?**	**Should police and criminals be allowed to date? (joke)**

Rank the top qualities you want in a boy / girlfriend

face, body, height, money, intelligence, snappy dresser

1. ____________
2. ____________
3. ____________
4. ____________

Rank the qualities you dislike the most

smoking, drinking, too poor, too short, unfaithful, violent, bad grammar in text messages

1. ____________
2. ____________
3. ____________
4. ____________

Why?
For example?

For example? Why exactly? When? Who? How? How long? What about you?

4 Shopping & Special Days

Shopping Personality

1. *Do you shop online* _____ *or on foot?* _____
2. *Do you get a weekly allowance* _____ *or beg every morning?* _____
3. *Do you shop around* _____ *or buy the first thing you find?* _____
4. *Do you prefer tight-fitting* _____ *or baggy clothes?* _____
5. *Do you plan what you wear* _____ *or throw anything on?* _____
6. *Is your father / mother cheap* _____ *or a big spender?* _____
7. *Is your mother a bargain shopper* _____ *or an impulse buyer?* _____
8. *What's your favorite sports brand?* ____________________
9. *What's your favorite fashion or cosmetics brand?* ____________________
10. *What's your favorite shopping district or department store?* ____________________

Really? *No way!* *Wow.* *Me too.* *Where?* *When?* *Who?* *How?*

Why? ***For example?*** ***What about you?***

Conversation Preparation

Do you prefer shopping online or on foot?

GUY *Hi. Long time no see. You look nice. Do you have a blind date after class?*

GAL *Well, A, thank you, and B, no date. It was my birthday last Saturday, and my mom took me out shopping for clothes.*

GUY *Well, A cool, and B, happy birthday. Did you do anything else for your birthday?*

GAL *No, shopping was it. All my friends were **cramming** for midterms, so we'll party later. My mom and I like shopping. For some people shopping is **hectic**, but not us. It's like **meditating** with money.*

GUY *Shopping? That's your thing? That's how you **relieve stress**?*

GAL *Yeah, I guess it's the female equivalent of computer games for guys. Visual stimulation.*

GUY *Oh, I get it now. Do you shop **online** or **on foot?***

GAL *Both, but I mainly prefer on foot.*

GUY *Why? It seems online is very **convenient**.*

GAL *True, but I prefer on foot. **First**, I already spend too much time in front of the computer, I need to get out and about. **Second**, colors and fabric are important to me, so I want to see that in person. What about you?*

GUY *Well, all fabric feels the same to me, and, frankly, I think I'm color blind.*

GAL *Too funny. And **third**, when I want something, I want it now. I don't want to wait three days.*

GUY *Ahh. **Instant gratification**.*

GAL *Yeah, that's me. And **finally**, I like to talk things over with the salesperson. They can be a big help.*

GUY *Sounds like you're a professional shopper. And hey, most of those salesgirls are very pretty.*

GAL *Anyway. Well, I take after my mom. She's a **bargain shopper**, big time. She only shops when there's a sale.*

GUY *Are you and your mother **brand conscious**?*

GAL *Oh, my mother is into luxury brands. Gucci, Prada, Chanel. Rolex.*

GUY *I've heard of Rolex, but those other names sound like animals to me. Sorry.*

GAL *You're thinking of a panda bear, not a Prada bear. Anyway. What's your favorite sports brand?*

Listen, repeat, record.
Listen to yourself.

GUY *For shoes I like Reebok, for everything else I like Nike.*

GAL *Do you shop online?*

GUY *Yeah, I much prefer shopping online. I don't like the crowds of shopping on foot. Online, it's **A**, stress free, **B**, big selection and **C,** lower prices. In sum, very convenient. What are you doing after school today?*

GAL *Birds gotta fly. Fish gotta swim. I gotta shop. It's my patriotic duty to help the economy.*

Write what you will say

Writing before Speaking improves Accuracy

This is writing practice. ***PUT SOME EFFORT INTO IT.***

1 **What did you do last weekend?** *Did you see any movies about shopping or birthdays?*
Last weekend I went shopping for some winter clothes at Lotte downtown, but I didn't see anything I liked.

____

2 **When's your birthday?** *What did you do on your last birthday?*
My birthday is on Halloween so we always have a costume party, or go to one. Last year I was Wonder Woman.

____

3 **If you were given $1000 what would you buy?** *Would you buy it for yourself or your sibling? (joke)*
I have two choices: A, buy a new iPhone or B, go to Japan for a week. I like to travel.

____

4 **Are you an impulse buyer?** *What is the last thing you bought?*
Yes, I'm an impulse buyer. I cannot control myself. I buy the stupidest stuff. My father says I need counselling.

____

5 **Is your mother a bargain shopper?** *Is your father a big spender?*
My mother is definitely a bargain shopper. She shops only when there are sales, and she has a million coupons.

____

6 **What's your favorite sport brand?** *What's your favorite fashion brand? Tech brand?*
For clothes and sports, I like Nike. For cosmetics, I like Chanel and Lancome. For tech, I like Apple.

____

7 **What's your next big purchase?** *Do you prefer to shop online or on foot?*
I want to get a new, stylish, heavy coat. Something long, warm, with a fur collar. I much prefer to shop on foot.

____

8 **What online shopping mall do you use?** *What department store is your favorite?*
To look for things, I go to Naver. They have the best search engine. Then, I go to Gmarket to buy it.

____

Really Me too Why? When? Where? Who? How often? How long?
Awesome Bummer Anyway Whatever Kind of It depends

Talk about what you wrote

Speaking to many partners improves Fluency

Make good, long sentences and try to use some new vocabulary.

9 Are birthdays big in your family? *Is Children's Day? Coming of age day? Homework day?*
Oh yes, my mother is into birthdays, and photos. She gets that from her side of the family. BIG birthday parties.

---

10 What's the last birthday party, party, graduation, festival, that you went to? *100 day? 70 year?*
Last month was busy. I went to my aunt's wedding and my first cousin's graduation.

---

11 If you were going to a costume party, which super hero would you dress as?
Some people use a costume party as an excuse to dress sexy, but I want to go as the Hulk and hit people.

---

12 Do you like going to weddings? *Do you like to skip the wedding and just go to the food?*
Weddings are OK. My parents have to go to a lot of them because they are managers at a big company.

---

13 Did you give or get anything on Valentine's Day? *White Day? Teacher's Day?*
I would like a gift on a special day that I can remember, but my boyfriend would rather go out and celebrate.

---

14 Did your parents have a big wedding? *Where was their honeymoon?*
My parents' wedding was HUGE. They both come from big families, and they're both first-born. They went to Bali.

---

15 What's your favorite holiday: Thanksgiving, Christmas, New Year, Chinese New Year?
I like New Year's, January first. We always go to the east coast to watch the sunrise. That's my father's thing.

---

16 What will you do after class? *What will you do this weekend? Any shopping plans this weekend?*
Saturday morning I will do my shopping research on the internet, and then go shopping in the afternoon.

For example? What about you?

Shopping Buffet

SHOPPING OPPOSITES

extras, like earphones, or earrings	**accessories**	1	**basics**	*food, clothes, rent, car*
has lots of extra room, very loose	**baggy**	2	**tight, skin tight**	*tight, very tight*
doesn't like to spend money	**cheap, frugal, thrifty**	3	**big spender**	*buys expensive things*
believes anything (lose 5 kilos in 1 day!)	**gullible**	4	**skeptical**	*does not believe, has doubts. 'No way!'*
bought today or this week	**brand new**	5	**used**	*it's already had one owner, maybe two*
real, authentic	**genuine**	6	**knock-off**	*copy, fake*
you want it now, can't wait	**instant gratification**	7	**delayed gratification**	*you can wait*
nice smelling stuff for women	**perfume**	8	**cologne**	*nice smelling stuff for men*
high-quality product	**prestige brand, brand name**	9	**generic**	*plain, OK, not fancy, not expensive*
shops only on sale days	**bargain shopper**	10	**impulse buyer**	*buys without thinking, regrets*
wears new, current designer styles	**stylish, trendy**	11	**out-of-style, tacky**	*clothes no one bought new*

12. **allowance** spending money you get from your parents. *My allowance is $50 per week.*
13. **bait and switch** attract you with one item or price and try to sell you a more expensive one.
14. **browse, browsing** to look around for shopping. *Can I help you? No thanks, I'm just browsing.*
15. **cheap** cheap is bad, low quality. Cheap merchandise is bad. However, a cheap price is good.
    This purse is cheap. Ten bucks! (good) A cheap person is bad. *My ex-boyfriend was cheap.* (bad)
16. **coming-of-age day** a traditional holiday to celebrate the age when you become an adult.
17. **fashionista** a female who is very stylish and into fashion. *She's a fashionista. Tres chic.* (French!)
18. **gyp, gypped** cheated, fooled. *This watch is a gyp. The hands never move. I got gypped.*
19. **haggle** to negotiate back and forth on the price. *My mom likes to haggle with the merchants.*
20. **luxury, luxury brand, luxurious** expensive and comfortable. *It's a luxury hotel. The rooms were luxurious.*
21. **one-stop shopping** a store, mall, or shopping center where you can buy everything, all in one place.
22. **receipt** (ree-seet) small piece of paper the cashier gives you that shows how much you paid.
23. **rip-off, ripped off** when you get charged way too much. *That place is a rip-off. I got ripped off.*
24. **shop till you drop** to shop so long that you are very tired. *I shopped till I dropped. I was exhausted.*
25. **shopaholic** an alcoholic drinks too much. A shopaholic loves to shop, and shops too much.
26. **shopping spree** when you go out and buy many things. *I went on a shopping spree for my birthday.*
27. **souvenir** something permanent (not food) you buy on vacation, for example, a t-shirt or coffee mug.
28. **splurge** to spend a lot, too much, but you deserve it. *It was my birthday so I splurged on myself.*
29. **tightwad** slang term for a very cheap person. *My uncle is a tightwad.*
30. **tourist trap** a store with no competition, for example, the only gift shop on a mountain top.
31. **variety, various** different kinds of items. *They have a variety of items. They have various kinds of food.*
32. **window shopping, eye shopping** to walk along and just look inside, through the window.

In America, on your birthday you leave your money at home. Your friends pay for everything.
Also, it's the tradition that the bride's father pays for the wedding.

Special Days Buffet

PARTIES
100-day, One year anniversary
birthday
graduation
Halloween
house-warming
retirement

1. **These pants are too:** long, short, tight, baggy, loose, wrinkled
2. **Your dress is too:** tight, short, low-cut, loose, baggy, long
3. **My heavy coat is:** thick, warm, waterproof, insulated. It has a hood.
4. **My jacket is:** light, thin, warm, reversible. It has a lot of pockets, zippers.
5. **Your blouse is:** thick, thin. It has horizontal, vertical stripes.
6. **Your sweater is:** turtleneck, V-neck, low-cut, unisex
7. **Her shoes are:** flats, low-heel, pumps, high-heel, platform, stiletto, open toe
8. **This weekend I will dress:** down, up, casual, dressy, depends on my mood

WEDDING TERMS
bride, groom *the male and female who get married*
bachelor / bachelorette party *wild party before the wedding for males / females*
best man / maid of honor *main male helper / main female helper*
wedding, wedding hall, wedding reception *the ceremony, the place, the food*
newlyweds *recently married*
traditional, religious wedding *according to tradition, or religion*
honeymoon *vacation after the wedding, hopefully to a romantic location*

WEDDING STUFF
flower bouquet
garter
prenuptial agreement
toasts
tuxedo
wedding dress, veil
wedding rings

Dress for success. Fake it till you make it.

Religious wedding

Traditional dress, untraditional behavior

Vocabulary Check

You will hear a short sentence with three possible answers, A, B, C. Mark the best answer with a big, black dot.

	1	2	3	4	5	6	7	8	9	10
A	O	O	O	O	O	O	O	O	O	O
B	O	O	O	O	O	O	O	O	O	O
C	O	O	O	O	O	O	O	O	O	O

1 Transcribe the quiz
2 Answer it
3 Check your answers

Longer Answers with Details

Focus! Make good, long sentences, and try to use some new vocabulary.

1. Longer writing is longer, smoother and better speaking.
2. You've never said these things before, so read, record and listen to yourself. *Put some feeling into it.*

1 What did you do on your last birthday? *Did you get a cake? Did you make a wish? What was it?*

2 What's the most expensive present that you ever got? *That you ever gave?*

3 Do you have any souvenirs from your travels? *What's your favorite? What place was your favorite?*

4 Did you ever get ripped off or gypped while shopping? *On vacation?*

New Year's Eve in Sydney, Australia

Graduation. *Yee ha!*

Answer in Academic Format

This can also be the start of your TOEFL Essay. Kill 2 birds with 1 stone.

Give specifics. It's your life, you know the details.

1 **What's your favorite sport or fashion brand? (Cosmetics, perfume, whatever) Or top 3 brands.**

*I like Puma. **First**, it's a name brand but it's not all over the place like Nike or Adidas. It's kind of unique. If I wear Nike, I feel like I'm advertising for them for free. **Second**, I like the way their clothes are designed. They're functional. If I ever get a girlfriend, I'd get us Puma campus couple jogging suits. **Third**, their clothes and shoes fit. I have a hard time finding shoes that fit just right. This weekend I'll get a new pair of Puma shoes.*

2 **Which of your parents is the cheapest, or the biggest spender?**

*That's easy, my mom is by far the cheapest. **First**, she shops only when there are sales. Any kind of sale: food, clothes, furniture, airline tickets, you name it. **Second**, she will surf the internet for hours just to save $1. You should hear her haggle with the merchants, especially when we are on vacation. **Third**, we get our Christmas presents the week after Christmas. This way she can get our stuff at the after-Christmas sales.*

For example? What about you?

Pronunciation Practice

Listen to yourself. *Are you getting better?* Why don't you do this in front of a mirror? Or video yourself?

i	æ	ɛ	I
seat	sat	set	sit
seed	sad	said	Sid
seen	san	sen	sin
least	last	lest	list
leave	laugh	lev	live
meet	mat	met	mitt

B	P	F	V
bew	pew	few	view
bile	pile	file	vile
bine	pine	fine	vine
bun	pun	fun	vun
by	pie	phi	vie
bail	pale	fail	veil

L	R	N	W
led	red	Ned	wed
leel	real	kneel	wheel
leer	near	rear	we're
len	ren	nin	when
life	rife	knife	wife
light	right	night	white

Th	T	D
those	toes	dose
though	toe	doe
thought	sought	taught
threw	true	drew
thy	tie	die
this	tis	dis

Descriptive Paragraph

1. Write your paragraph on computer, put your photo on it, and glue or staple it here.
2. Answer any question in the unit. Answer in detail, something you want to talk about.
3. **EXTRA POINTS if you include a photo. Double extra points if you are in the photo.**

How was your last birthday? Or. Are birthdays big in your family?

My last birthday was awesome. My friends took me out (American style, they paid) to Outback. Also, my father always adds a $100 bill to my ***allowance*** *on my birthday. So, my friends* ***treated*** *me to Outback, and I treated them to a sports bar after. Ireland was playing Scotland and they absolutely could not understand the announcers' accents. My English professor is from Scotland so I was able to translate. Good times. I kept the receipts and framed them, and put them on my wall as souvenirs. We took a lot of* ***selfies,*** *and some are on my wall. I put a bunch of photos on my Facebook page. From the photos you can watch the progression of our drinking. Too funny. My mother took me shopping for my birthday, which is unusual because normally she's a* ***bargain shopper*** *and shops only on sale days. She said I need some good* ***casual clothes*** *for school, and she knows clothes. She bought me some* ***dressy jeans*** *and polo* ***shirts****. I begged a little, and she got me some Nike tennis shoes. Nike has such a* ***wide variety*** *of shoes, it was hard to choose. She also bought me some wireless earphones, which are now a* ***necessity*** *rather than an* ***accessory****. My mom is into* ***one-stop shopping****, so that was* ***convenient****. All in all, it was a great birthday. Great parents, good friends, and new clothes. All I need now is a girlfriend. And an iPhone 12 to call her with.*

TOEFL Essay

Answer a conversation question with a TOEFL essay.

Follow the example and write your own. ***Write something that interests you!***

Write about what interests you. Use any question in this unit. Below are other possibilities.

If I were given $1000, I would buy A, B, C.
I'm an impulse buyer because of A, B, C.
My last birthday was awesome because

My favorite sport brands are A, B, C.
My favorite fashion brand is
My favorite shopping district is

My favorite holiday is because A, B, C.
My father is a big spender because
My mother is frugal because

A15 Amy Lawrence

Do you prefer shopping online or on foot?

My father, mother, and I have very different personalities, and we have different ways of shopping. My father shops online. My mother shops on foot to find what she wants and then buys it online, and I like to shop in person. For my father, shopping is a chore. For mom, it's her job to get the best and pay the least, and me, I just like walking around and the experience.

First, my father is a ***discriminating consumer***. He does extensive research online before buying anything. He searches Google and reads reviews, lots of reviews, especially for electronics. Some electronics are much cheaper on amazon, but the shipping to Asia is expensive. So, he buys from Amazon and has it shipped to his sister in California, and she mails it here. Also, he buys used books in America, for $2 or $3 and the shipping is $16. So, he gets a nearly-new book for less than $20. He much prefers a book he can put on the shelf more than an E-book.

Second, my mother is a champion shopper. She'll go out and find the products she wants in a store and examines them carefully. And take pictures. Then, she'll come home and buy them on the internet. She waits until she needs a lot of things and orders them at the same time, that way she gets free shipping. She's also very ***picky***. If some fruit or something is not fresh, she'll call them and send them back.

Third, I like shopping on foot with my friends. It's like a social experience. I like being out and about instead of ***cooped up*** at home in front of a computer screen. I like shopping downtown because it's centrally located and easy to get there. Also, there are several universities nearby, and most stores ***cater to*** college kids. It's crucial to me to get the right size and color. I hate it when I get something online that doesn't fit and the color is off. Then, it's a ***hassle*** to return it. No thanks.

Well, there it is. My father shops online. He likes the ability to research and to find the best item at the lowest price, and he's not bothered if it takes a week or so to get. My mom is a professional shopper. She takes pride in getting the best for least. And if there were a contest for haggling, she would probably win. Me, I like being out and about and shopping on foot. I like the social experience. (424 words)

Dad in shopping mode

Mom researching

Me socializing & shopping

Just do it.

Yes, it's homework,
but it's about YOU!
Get into it.

WRAP PARTY!

PERSONALITY	BIRTHDAYS	PARTIES	MONEY
Is your father / mother cheap or a big spender? *Are they cheap about certain things?*	**When's your birthday?** *What did you do on your last birthday?*	**If you were going to a costume party, which superhero would you go as?**	**Did you ever loan money to a friend?** *Did you ever borrow? Details please.*
Would you rather be house rich and cash poor, or vice-versa? *For example?*	**What's the most expensive present you ever got? What's the most expensive present you ever gave?**	**What was the last wedding you went to?** *Are they still married? (joke)*	**How much is your allowance?** *Do you have your own savings account?*
Do you buy the first thing you find, or shop around a while? *For example?*	**What's the earliest birthday you remember?** *Details please.*	**Do you spend a lot of time getting dressed, or do you just throw anything on?**	**Did you ever have a part-time job?** *How long did it last? Were you ever fired?*
How many credit cards do you have? *Did you ever lose one?*	**What's the best Children's Day you ever had?**	**When you go out with friends, do you prefer to dress up or dress down?**	**Do your grandparents give you money on New Years?**
Is your mother a bargain shopper? *Does she shop only when there are sales?*	**Are birthdays big in your family?** *For example?*	**Did you ever dress up for a Halloween or costume party?** *What did you wear?*	**If you could have any kind of car, what would it be?**

List your top 4 sport brands

Nike, Reebok, Adidas, North Face
Puma, Under Armour, Converse

1. ____________
2. ____________
3. ____________
4. ____________

Your top 4 clothing & fashion brands

Levis, Ralph Lauren, Calvin Klein
Prada, Dior, Armani, Chanel

1. ____________
2. ____________
3. ____________
4. ____________

Use this to start conversations.

What's your . . . ?

For example? Why exactly? How much? When? Where? What about you?

When's your birthday?

PERSONALITY	SHOPPING	HOLIDAYS	TECH
Do you prefer a high-priced brand name, or will generic do?	Did you ever buy a fake by mistake? *Details please.*	Did you get anything expensive for high school graduation? *A car? Trip to Paris?*	What kind of computer do you have? *Do you have your own printer?*
Does your mother or father haggle with the merchant?	What's your favorite department store? *Why?*	Did you ever get ripped off while shopping or on vacation? *Details please.*	What kind of phone do you have? *Did you ever use your phone in an emergency?*
Do you prefer to shop online or on foot? *For example?*	Would you ever buy anything used? *For example?*	What was the last party, concert or game you went to?	How many phones have you had in your life? *How old is your phone? Did you ever lose a phone?*
What site do you use when you shop online?	Did you ever have to wear hand-me-down clothes?	Did you get or give anything on White Day, or Valentines Day?	What's your next tech purchase? *How much will you spend?*
What part of town do you usually go shopping in?	Does your mother buy groceries online? *Is she high tech?*	Does your mother drag you to family weddings or do you want to go?	Do you buy books online or at a bookstore? *Where? Why?*

List the top 4 personal improvements on your wish list

Looks, brains, personality, body, hair, taller, thinner, better dancer, not so shy, smaller ears, better at sports. *Nothing, I'm perfect.*

1. ______________
2. ______________
3. ______________
4. ______________

Your next 4 purchases

phone, laptop, computer, printer, wireless earphones, heavy coat, dress, pants, shoes, purse, watch, earrings, ring, backpack, tattoo

1. ______________
2. ______________
3. ______________
4. ______________

Why?

For example? Why exactly? How much? When? Where? What about you?

5 Health & Happiness

Healthy & Happy Personality

1. *Are you an action figure* ______ *or a couch potato?* ______
2. *Are you happy alone* ______ *or in a crowd?* ______
3. *When you're in pain, do you whine* ______ *or suffer in silence?* ______
4. *Are you a junk food junkie* ______ *or a healthy eater?* ______
5. *Do you crave chocolate* ______ *or chips?* ______
6. *Is your mother / father, an idea person* ______ *or a detail person* ______
7. *Which does your family try first: Chinese* ______ *or Western medicine?* ______
8. *Would you rather be: taller?* ______ *thinner ?* ______ *or rich?* ______
9. *What makes you happiest: food?* ______ *friends?* ______ *or grades?* ______
10. *What gives you the most stress: parents?* ______ *professors?* ______ *commuting?* ______

Me too! Why? For example? What about you?

Conversation Preparation

Are you a happy camper? Are you a healthy camper?

It hurts when I smile. Stop smiling.

GUY *Hi. How's it going? You're looking great today.*

GAL *Why thank you! Wait. I think I heard you say that to your last partner.*

GUY *Oh, I say that to everybody. You'd be amazed at how happy it makes people feel. My father is in sales.*

GAL *Oh, I get it now. Well, anyway, thanks. So, are you always happy? Do you ever* ***get the blues****?*

GUY *I'm always happy. I was kind of a sickly child. I was* ***allergic*** *to a lot of things, but now I'm a lean, mean healthy machine. What about you?*

GAL *What about me? Am I always happy or always healthy?*

GUY *Your choice.*

GAL *Both. They're related. Luckily, I get healthy* ***genes*** *from my parents. They're both happy, optimistic people. They look on the bright side of everything. Even when I make low grades. What about you?*

GUY *Lucky you. Let's see, my family's medical history. My mom is the boss there. She thinks that,* ***first****, a good diet is the key to health, and* ***second****, health and fitness are the key to happiness. And* ***third****, she says that sleep is more important than studying. And that makes me REAL happy.*

GAL *Your mom is very smart. If I'm tired while studying, I don't remember a thing. It was a waste of time.*

GUY *I know what you mean. Did you ever miss school because you were sick?*

GAL *Yes, one time I had the* ***flu,*** *bad. I stayed home for a week. I did not feel bad, but I was* ***contagious*** *and they did not want me spreading anything around school. What about you? Were you ever sick or injured?*

GUY *I cut my arm, kind of badly, when I fell off my bike and onto a fence.*

GAL *Ouch. I bet that hurt. How many* ***stitches****? Do you have a* ***scar****? Did you cry?*

GUY *I never cry. My dad is the* ***strong, silent type****. Real men don't cry. I got a bunch of* ***stitches****, but no scar. They have some really good* ***ointments*** *these days for that.*

Just do it.

GAL *Did your mom panic when she saw the* ***blood****?*

GUY *No, not at all. She comes from a large family, she's the oldest of seven kids, and I guess she saw a lot of that when she was growing up.*

GAL *Is your family into exercise?*

GUY *Yes. My parents belong to a* ***health club*** *and go three times a week. My mother does Jazzercise and yoga, and my father does* ***weights*** *and the* ***Nordic machine****. What about you?*

GAL *My mom is into healthy cooking. She makes me watch cooking shows with her. They're in English. She says we can kill two birds with one stone: learn cooking and English. If the university entrance exam was about cooking* ***recipes****, I'd be at Harvard right now.*

Write what you will say

Writing before Speaking improves Accuracy

This is writing practice. *PUT SOME EFFORT INTO IT.*

1 **What did you do last weekend?** *What did you do on Sunday? What did you do last winter?*
Last weekend my parents joined a health club. So I went with them while they got a tour of all the facilities.

2 **Have you ever missed school because you were sick or injured?** *Were you really sick?*
No, I'm healthy as a horse. I never get sick. That runs in my family, we are all super healthy.

3 **Do you have any allergies? Are you allergic to anything?** *Dogs, cats, shellfish, homework?*
I used to have sinus allergies every spring, but not anymore. My sister is allergic to crabs and oysters.

4 **Do your parents belong to a health club?** *Do they swim, do weights, stretch, dance?*
Yes, my mom goes everyday to a stretching class. My father started out strong but stopped going.

5 **Do you wear contacts?** *Did you ever wear braces? Did you ever get a really bad haircut?*
I wear contacts to play sports, but usually I wear my glasses. I hope to get LASIK later.

6 **Does your family use Chinese medicine?** *Is that Plan A or B?*
My uncle likes acupuncture. He swears by it. And he drinks some kind of expensive green tea from Japan.

7 **When you're sick, do you complain a lot, or suffer in silence?**
I rarely get sick but when I do, I get all worried and, well, I complain a lot. I bother my mom at work.

8 **Were you ever in an accident?** *Did you ever break a bone, get burned, or get cut badly?*
I was in a minor accident two years ago. Somebody ran a red light. I just got a bruised forehead.

Really Me too Why? When? Where? Who? How often? How long?
Awesome Bummer Anyway Whatever Kind of It depends

Talk about what you wrote

Speaking to many partners improves Fluency

Make good, long sentences and try to use some new vocabulary.

9 Do you like sports and exercise? *What's your favorite? Did you ever win an athletic contest?*
Yes, my whole family is into fitness and sports. I took taekwondo for six years, and now I play tennis.

____

10 How often does your family eat out? *How often do you get food delivered?*
My father is a foodie. He loves to try new places. We eat out about twice a week. And we get Chinese delivered.

____

11 Did you ever eat food that made you sick? *Are you a picky eater?*
Once on vacation, the whole family got sick. My father likes to try the local food. Well, he used to.

____

12 Do you watch your weight, or eat whatever you want whenever you want?
Actually, I used to weigh 10 kilos more. I finally decided that I have to go hungry all the time to stay in shape.

____

13 Do your parents drink a lot of coffee? *Do you drink coffee? Did you ever have an energy drink?*
My father drinks a lot of coffee, but none on vacation. Talk about a difference. He's more mellow on vacation.

____

14 How do your parents relieve stress? *How do you give them stress? How do they give you stress?*
My mother likes to read, and my father likes fishing and camping. That takes a lot of planning, but he likes it.

____

15 Is your family naturally healthy or do they have to work at it by eating healthy and exercising?
Half and half. My father's side never gets sick. My mother's side has high cholesterol and gets gray hair early.

____

16 What will you do after school? *What will you do this weekend?*
This weekend we'll go see my grandmother. It's her big 80th birthday. That's a lot of candles.

____

For example? What about you?

Health Buffet

HEALTH PERSONALITY

always doing something, energetic	**active**	1	**couch potato**	*watches a lot of TV*
a happy, cheerful person	**happy camper**	2	**unhappy camper**	*not happy*
in good health, healthy, looks good	**in shape**	3	**out of shape**	*gets tired easily, walking up stairs*
likes being outdoors	**outdoors person**	4	**indoors person**	*likes staying indoors, reading, TV*
eats healthy, eats nutritious food	**healthy eater**	5	**junk food junkie**	*loves junk food, eats a lot*
high opinion of yourself	**high self-esteem**	6	**low self-esteem**	*low opinion, feel unworthy*
a waterfall, a sleeping puppy	**relaxed**	7	**stressed**	*rap music, a dentist office*
to endure pain quietly	**suffer in silence**	8	**whine, complain a lot**	*complain long and loud*

9. **ache / hurt / sore** slight pain. *I ache. My arm aches. I hurt my arm. My arm hurts. My arm is sore.*
10. **acupuncture** Chinese medicine where they stick tiny needles into you.
11. **acne, pimple** a little boil or volcano on your face. *Oh no! Class picture day and I have a pimple on my nose.*
12. **addicted, addiction** to need something very much. *I'm addicted to coffee. She has a chocolate addiction.*
13. **allergic, allergy, allergic reaction** your body does not like something. *I'm allergic to dust. I have an allergy. I get a sinus allergy every spring. I had an allergic reaction to that shellfish.*
14. **blood type: A, B, AB, O negative, positive** blood comes in several types. *My blood type is O negative.*
15. **bruise, black and blue** your body is slightly damaged. *I bruised my arm. It was black and blue for a week.*
16. **dizzy** crazy feeling after you spin around three times. *Whoa, I studied too hard, I'm dizzy.*
17. **faint / pass out / black out** lose consciousness. Women faint, men pass out, and black out. *He blacked out.*
18. **genes** DNA from your parents. *I have good genes. All my family is tall and thin. We can eat whatever.*
19. **nauseous, nauseated** bad feeling before you throw up. *I'm nauseous. I'm nauseated. I feel nauseated.*
20. **quality time** good, one-on-one time with someone. *I had some quality time with my father last weekend.*
21. **rash** red, itchy skin, usually because you are allergic. *I had a rash. I have a skin rash. It itches.*
22. **rewarding, fulfilling, satisfaction** you get mental pleasure from it. *Doing volunteer work is rewarding. My mother gets a lot of satisfaction from helping out at the old folks home.*
23. **runs in the family** it's common in your family. *Diabetes runs in the family. Music ability runs in our family.*
24. **scar** a mark on the skin after you heal. *I cut my arm, and here is the scar. I have a scar on my leg.*
25. **shot / injection** a needle they stick in you to deliver drugs. *I got a shot in arm. They gave me an injection.*
26. **sinuses** cavity, hollow space behind your nose. *Pollen and dust hurt them. My sinuses are bothering me.*
27. **sprain** your leg or arm is bent, but not broken. *I sprained my ankle playing basketball.*
28. **stitches** after you are cut, they sew you up with thread. *I cut my arm and got stitches.*
29. **strong silent type** does not show pain or emotion. *My father is the strong silent type.*
30. **throw up, vomit** food comes out of your mouth. *I threw up. I vomited. It was something I ate.*
31. **swelling, swollen** gets bigger. *I twisted my ankle, and there was swelling. It was swollen.*
32. **walk-in-clinic > emergency room > hospital > specialist** order in which you might seek help.

Food Buffet

FOOD OPPOSITES

a little food before the meal	**appetizer**	1	**dessert**	*eaten after the meal, pastry*
tastes like water	**bland**	2	**spicy**	*a strong, hot taste*
makes noise when you eat, crunchy	**crispy**	3	**greasy**	*sticky, oily, red sauce*
makes you fat	**high calorie**	4	**low calorie**	*boring taste*
healthy	**nutritious**	5	**junk food**	*chocolate, pastry, candy*
does not like many foods	**picky eater**	6	**eat anything**	*all food tastes great*

1. **atmosphere** The mood. TGIF has a festive atmosphere. Outback has an Aussie mood.
2. **binge, binge eating or drinking** To take in a whole lot, but not that often.
3. **crave, craving** To want something badly. Some people crave desert after a big meal.
4. **foodie** Somebody who likes to try different kinds of food.
5. **freebie** You get something free: appetizer, cola. Regular customers often get this.
6. **leftovers** Food left over from the night or day before.
7. **midnight munchies** When you get hungry late at night and need a snack.
8. **pig out** To eat very much, until you are full, stuffed, pants about to burst.
9. **stuffed** How you feel after you ate too much. Like a big stuffed bear.
10. **vegetarian, vegan** Does not eat meat, might eat fish.

ETHNIC FOOD
Chinese
Greek
Indian
Italian
Japanese
Korean
Mexican
Thai
Vietnamese

SWEETS
cake
candy
chocolate
dessert
donuts
ice cream
pastry
pie
pudding

Fitness freak by day

Midnight munchies by night

Vocabulary Check

You will hear a short sentence with three possible answers, A, B, C. Mark the best answer with a big, black dot.

	1	2	3	4	5	6	7	8	9	10
A	O	O	O	O	O	O	O	O	O	O
B	O	O	O	O	O	O	O	O	O	O
C	O	O	O	O	O	O	O	O	O	O

1 Transcribe the quiz
2 Answer it
3 Check your answers

Longer Answers with Details

Focus! Make good, long sentences, and try to use some new vocabulary.

1. Longer writing is longer, smoother, and better speaking.
2. You've never said these things before, so read, record, and listen to yourself. *Put some feeling into it.*

1 Tell me about the last time you exercised or played a sport. *Can you remember?*

____

____

____

2 Tell me about your worst sickness or injury. *Did it hurt? Were you scared? Who saved you?*

____

____

____

3 What's your favorite food? *Favorite junk food? Favorite restaurant? Favorite kind of food?*

____

____

____

4 How do you relax? How do you relieve stress? Who gives you the most stress?

____

____

____

Things that cause stress

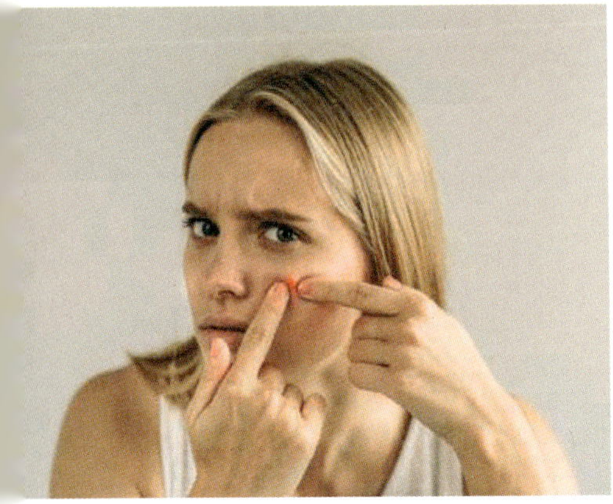

Indoor person relieving stress

Outdoor person relieving stress

Answer in Academic Format

This will improve your speaking, essays, and presentations.

Take your time. Look up some advanced words if you like.

1 **What are the top three things that cause you stress? What do you worry about?**

First, I'm stressed about school and my grades. I dropped a required class because I was doing so badly. I'll have to take it again this winter. Second, I take the subway two hours a day to and from school. It's crowded with stressed and busy people. I hope I can live in the dorm next semester. Third, my friends like to drink and smoke, and want me to, but I don't like that behavior. I may have to find new friends.

____

____

____

____

2 **How do your parents relax? Does your family do any sports or exercise together?**

My parents are the outdoors type, and they relax by getting outdoors. First, about once a month, we all go hiking up a mountain. Mom packs a lunch, and we make a day trip out of it. Luckily, Mom is a detail person. Second, my dad likes to fish, and my mom goes along to read. He gets upset if she catches more fish than him. Third, they belong to a health club. They go twice a week and are taking a ballroom dancing course.

____

____

____

____

For example? What about you?

Pronunciation Practice

Japanese and French accents sound different. *Why?* They use different muscles. Muscles require practice.

i	æ	ɛ	ɪ
meet	mat	met	mitt
neat	nat	net	knit
peet	pat	pet	pit
reed	rad	red	rid
seat	sat	set	sit
seed	sad	said	Sid

L	R	N	W
lock	rock	nock	wok
low	row	no	woe
lack	rack	nack	wack
late	rate	Nate	wait
lay	ray	nay	way
lead	read	need	weed

pool	pull
fool	full
noon	none
dune	done
oops	ups
goon	gun
poop	pup

loyal	royal
national	rational
legal	regal
leader	reader
lower	rower
laser	razor
list	wrist

Descriptive Paragraph

1. Answer any question in the unit. Answer in detail, something you want to talk about.
2. **EXTRA POINTS if you include a photo. Double extra points if you're in the photo.**

Something about Health

I am generally pretty healthy. I broke my leg when I was seven. I was jumping into the pool, but I missed the pool. Actually, I am pretty sure that I was pushed, but I have no proof. Anyway. I hurt pretty bad for a while and my leg was ***black and blue*** *by the time we got to the hospital. Then they put a* ***cast*** *on it, and it was OK. I wore the* ***cast*** *for about two months. All my friends wrote their name on my cast, so that was pretty cool. Otherwise, I rarely* ***catch a cold*** *and when I do it is not too* ***severe****.*

My older sister has ***sinus*** *problems with* ***pollen*** *every spring. Her eyes water, and it looks like she's upset about her boyfriend, but she says it's just her* ***sinuses****. She wore braces in middle school and she hated that, but she loves her teeth now. She wears glasses and* ***contacts****, and she'll get* ***LASIK*** *surgery this winter. She can't wait. Her body had an* ***allergic reaction*** *to contacts, so she does not wear them anymore.*

Good ***genes run in our family****. We are all tall, fit, and healthy, and my parents think that health and well-being are important. My mom says "Unhealthy students cannot study for hours and hours so you guys stay healthy!" She and dad belong to a health club and go three times a week. Dad goes swimming, and mom goes to the stretching class. They are both in pretty* ***good shape*** *and they signed up to run a* ***half-marathon*** *this winter. My two sisters and I are going to dress up as Marvel Super heros and cheer them on near the finish line.*

TOEFL Essay

Answer a conversation question with a TOEFL essay. You know the drill.

What you write about is what you're going to talk about in class, and on your conversation test.

So write about something that interests you! Use any question from the unit, and here are some others:

1. *How does your family stay healthy?*
2. *How does each member of your family stay healthy and happy? Stress free?*
3. *What's your family's biggest health problem?*
4. *How will you improve your health and well-being this year?*
5. *How does your favorite sport or exercise keep you healthy and happy?*
6. *What gives you stress? How do you get rid of stress?*

Just do it.

A15 Amy Lawrence

About Heath, Food and Fitness

My family is very healthy, and I can prove it. Health and well-being, mind and body are very important to my mother. She says she leaves the wealth up to dad. She doesn't mind him being a workaholic, but she wants him to be a healthy one. We are healthy because of our mindset, diet, and exercise.

First, both my parents strongly believe that happiness is the key to health. The body follows the mind. Every morning my mom wakes us up by yelling, "Is everybody a ***happy camper*** today!" Too funny. She watches a lot of the medical shows on TV that talk about health problems. She thinks that stress is bad, so she never pushes us too much about our grades. She's big into ***preventative*** measures, like exercise. Healthy habits that prevent sickness are better than medicine to ***cure***. And my father's motto is: "Happy wife, happy life."

Second, my mother thinks that a good diet is the key to good health. She uses all fresh ingredients when she cooks, and she never lets us eat ***processed food*** that comes in a bag, like ramen or chips. She spends a lot of time cooking, but she calls it a ***labor of love***. She knows which restaurants in the area have the healthiest food, and we get food delivered about once a week. And every weekend we go to a ***buffet*** or restaurant that has a good salad buffet. My father likes Dominos best.

Finally, while my mom is into happiness and food, my dad is into exercise. He works hard and he plays hard. He goes to the health club on his way home from work and mainly does the Nordic track. He says he works off the ***stress*** of the day before coming home. Of course, he ***rewards*** the workout with a glass of wine after supper. He used to drink beer and soju, but now it's red wine. My sister and I are pretty ***active***. She likes jazzercise and yoga, and I play soccer and tennis. We take a big skiing vacation every year. We're all fit.

Therefore, you can see that my family is happy and healthy. My mom is like a ***morale officer*** in the army, always making sure we're feeling good. Her ***motto*** is: if you're not in a good mood, stay in your room. She also makes sure we eat well. It's like her second job. And my father thinks that exercise is key. Working out ***strenuously*** relieves a lot of stress. My motto is: happy, healthy parents = happy life. (418 words)

That's me at Muju. A well-dressed wannabe.

Mom in cooking mode. Using the phone and internet seems kind of like cheating somehow.

My dad sipping wine. At home his wine glass is much bigger.

VOCABULARY

happy	processed food	stress
preventative	labor of love	rewards
cure	morale officer	active
	motto	strenuously

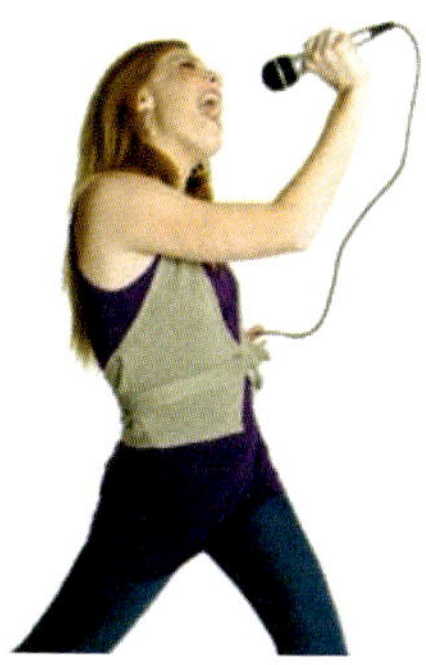

Yes, it's homework, but it's about YOU! *Get into it.*

WRAP PARTY!

PERSONALITY	FOOD	HEALTH	FAMILY
Do you suffer in silence or complain a lot? *For example?*	**Did you ever eat food that made you sick?** *Are you allergic to any foods?*	**Which movie star do you think has had the most plastic surgery?** *Who do you suspect?*	**Does any health condition run in your family?** *Laziness? Joke.*
Is your mother cool in a crisis or does she over-react? *For example?*	**What's your favorite junk food?** *What's your favorite home delivery food?*	**Do you have any scars or birthmarks?** *Are you self-conscious about it?*	**What gives you the most stress: parents, siblings, money or grades?**
Are you a healthy eater or a junk food junky? *For example?*	**How much coffee do you drink per day?** *Do you use coffee to study?*	**Did you ever get sick on vacation?** *Eat some bad food?*	**How many of your grandparents are still alive?** *Where do they live?*
Are you healthy as a horse or sometimes sick? *For example?*	**How often does your family eat out? Where?** *How often does your family get food delivered?*	**Were you ever in a car accident?** *Were you ever burned or badly cut?*	**Does your family use Chinese medicine?** *Acupuncture?*
Do you prefer a large amount of cheap food or a small amount of expensive food?	**Did you ever go on a diet?** *What kind of diet? How long did it last?*	**Do you know any first aid?** *Did you ever help anyone in distress?*	**Do your parents belong to a health club?** *Are they into fitness?*

Did you ever?
✓ for yes, X for no

1. Play tennis ______
2. Play golf ______
3. Go fishing ______
4. Sky dive ______
5. Bungee jump ______
6. Go white-water rafting ______
7. Camp overnight ______
8. Go fishing ______

Can you?

1. Swim ______
2. Ski ______
3. Snowboard ______
4. Ice skate ______
5. Rollerblade ______
6. Skateboard ______
7. Scuba dive ______

Total ______

For example? When? Who? How long? What about you?

Are you a happy camper?

PERSONALITY	HEALTH	STRESS	EXERCISE
Did you ever help an injured person? *Did you ever accidently injure a person?*	**Did you ever have a big memory gap after drinking alcohol?**	**How do your parents relax?** *How do they give you stress?*	**What's your favorite sport or exercise?** *How often do you do it? Are you good at it?*
Is your father the strong silent type, or does he express his emotions?	**Do you have any scars? Multiple earrings?** *Tattoos? Six toes?*	**What's the greatest danger you've ever been in?**	**How many hours do you sleep every night?** *What time do you wake up, and go to bed?*
What's your blood type? *Do you believe it's related to personality type?*	**Did you ever think about getting LASIK surgery?** *Do you know anyone who's had it?*	**Would you like to be a doctor, nurse, or pharmacist?**	**Were you ever injured while exercising?** *Details please.*
Are you accident-prone or never injured?	**Did you ever faint or pass out?** *Get dizzy?*	**How many hours a week do you spend on homework?** *(Or, how many minutes.) Joke*	**How often do you get quality time with your father, mother?**
Are you an action figure or a couch potato?	**Would you rather be: taller, smarter, thinner, or better looking?**	**Did you ever lie about being sick and try to miss school?**	**Did you ever miss school because you were sick or injured?**

What are the top 3 things that give you stress?

1. __________
2. __________
3. __________

The top 3 things that relieve your stress?

1. __________
2. __________
3. __________

Your top 3 foods?

1. __________
2. __________
3. __________

Why?

For example? When? Who? How long? What about you?

6 Festivals & Getting There

Festive Personality

1.	*Is your family the indoors*	______	*or outdoors type?*	______
2.	*Does your father have a lot of patience*	______	*or a short fuse?*	______
3.	*Does your family travel light*	______	*or do you pack everything?*	______
4.	*Are you a light sleeper*	______	*or a heavy sleeper?*	______
5.	*Are your parents well-organized*	______	*or every trip is chaos?*	______
6.	*Does your father like the scenic route*	______	*or he goes straight there?*	______
7.	*Would you rather go to a water park*	______	*or a snow festival?*	______
8.	*Would you prefer camping*	______	*or staying at the Hilton?*	______
9.	*Does your family always arrive on time*	______	*or usually get there late?*	______
10.	*Are your parents early birds*	______	*or night owls?*	______

Me too! Why? For example? What about you?

Conversation Preparation

What festival is on your bucket list?

GUY *Hi. How's it going? Are you ready for this semester to end?*

GAL *Oh yeah. Big time. And you?*

GUY *Me too. What will you do this weekend?*

GAL *We're going to the countryside for a flower festival. I forget the name. I'd look it up, but, you know, my phone is over there on the professor's desk.*

GUY *Yeah. Ditto. How will you go?*

GAL *Oh, my father has a new* ***SUV****. He loves that thing. We go somewhere every weekend. He's like a kid with a new toy. Whenever we get on the* ***expressway*** *he yells Yeee-Hah! like a cowboy on a horse.*

GUY *Too funny. Is your father a good driver?*

GAL *He's a good driver, but he's not a quiet driver. It's like he's a tour guide. He talks and talks, and he reads out loud all the signs we pass. One day he'll realize that my brother and I have our earphones on.*

GUY *Not my father. It's like he's an airline pilot, all focused. Anyway. Is your family* ***into*** *festivals?*

GAL *Oh, I love festivals and theme parks. My favorite is Caribbean Bay. What about you?*

GUY *My favorite is Universal Studios in Osaka. That place is awesome.*

GAL *You've been there? Lucky you. Why do you like it?*

GUY ***First****, I'm into Harry Potter, and they have an exhibit, and I bought a wand there.* ***Second****, their Jurassic Park is awesome.* ***Third****, the Spider-Man exhibit. Those are the top three, but there are many more. If you ever get a chance, you should definitely go there. On a scale of one to ten, it's a ten. Absolutely.*

GAL *Wow. You're a big fan. Will you travel anywhere this winter?*

GUY *Yes, we're going to Thailand to celebrate New Year's, and I'm really* ***looking forward to*** *that. Is your father* ***spontaneous****?*

GAL *Big time. If he hears about something interesting on Friday, we head out on Saturday. He says real men don't need to plan in advance.*

Just do it.

GUY *My father's like that. How are your grades this semester?*

GAL *Not too good. I* ***fell behind*** *right before midterm and never* ***caught up****. This winter I'm going to* ***recharge my batteries*** *and make straight A's next semester. How about your grades?*

GUY *Don't ask. I get* ***depressed*** *even thinking about them. This semester started out so well. Then I joined a club and got a girlfriend, and got a job to take out my girlfriend, and there went my grades.*

GAL ***Bummer****. Well, you wanted a girlfriend. You know the saying: "When the gods want to punish you, they give you what you want."*

GUY *Oh yeah. Well, why didn't the gods take my girlfriend and leave me good grades?*

Write what you will say

Writing before Speaking improves Accuracy

This is writing practice. *PUT SOME EFFORT INTO IT.*

1 **What did you do last weekend?**
Last weekend my father took us camping on the east coast. Actually, I'm not sure where we were.

2 **Did you go to any festivals this year?** *What festival do you really want to go to?*
I went to Mardi Gras in New Orleans. It was awesome: food, music, dancing, parades. People acting crazy.

3 **What's your favorite theme park?** *What theme parks did you go to this year?*
I like Universal Studios in Osaka. That place has everything. And Japan is so neat and organized.

4 **Do your parents like festivals? Theme parks?** *Do they like to escape the city on weekends?*
My father is like a big kid. He loves festivals and parks more than most kids. His enthusiasm is infectious.

5 **What does your family do for Chuseok?** *What do you do for the Lunar New Year?*
We go to Daegu where my oldest uncle lives. We leave at midnight, so we sleep while my father drives.

6 **What's the most adventurous thing you've ever done?** *White-water rafting? Bungee jump?*
My school club went white-water rafting last summer, and I rode an elephant in Thailand.

7 **Is your father a city boy or a country boy? Is your mother a city or country girl?**
My father is a city boy, but my mother's brother is a country boy, so his family always goes camping with us.

8 **What's your dream car?** *What color? Do you want a chick magnet?*
Oh, I would like a bright red Porsche. Convertible. Chick magnet. Like in the movie Sixteeen Candles.

Really Me too Why? When? Where? Who? How often?
Anyway Whatever Kind of Half and half It depends

Talk about what you wrote

Speaking to many partners improves Fluency

Make good, long sentences and try to use some new vocabulary.

9 What will you do this winter vacation? *Have you ever traveled abroad?*
I'm going to bike ride around Jeju Island with some high school friends. It might take two or three weeks.

____

10 How are your grades this semester? *What was your hardest class? Your easiest class?*
My grades were OK, nothing to brag about. My hardest class was Theory of Accounting. They lost me on day one.

____

11 Do you know what courses you will take next semester? *Did you drop any classes this semester?*
I know the courses I will take, I just don't know what day or time they will be. I hate to quit. I'll never drop a class.

____

12 Which do you like more, your major or your club? *What's your dream job? What's your Plan B?*
Actually, my club. I'm thinking of staying out a year to get a better grade so I can change my major.

____

13 Did you make any new friends this semester? This year? *Did you make any enemies?*
I met a lot of nice people but I still mainly hangout with my high school friends. Maybe this semester.

____

14 Where do you live? *Do you live in a high rise, a villa or what? What floor?*
I live in a high-rise complex in Ilsan. We live on the 27th floor. We have a great view of the next building.

____

15 Tell me about your neighborhood. *Is there much to do? Do you hang out there or near school?*
I live in a big, new apartment complex. Everything is shiny and new. I mainly hang out near school.

____

16 What will you do after class? *What will you do this weekend?*
After class my major club is going to the countryside to do volunteer work. Back to nature with bugs and mud.

____

For example? What about you?

Vocabulary Buffet

OUTDOOR OPPOSITES

		#		
likes action, thrills, excitement / *likes action, adventure, danger*	**action addict** / **adrenaline junkie**	1	**couch potato**	*watches a lot of TV on the sofa*
spends as little as possible	**cheap, frugal**	2	**big spender**	*likes to travel first class, spend money*
wakes up very early, 4 - 5 a.m.	**early bird**	3	**night owl**	*stays up very late, till 3 - 4 a.m.*
enjoyed very much, want to do again	**hooked on**	4	**never again**	*was not enjoyable, once was enough*
likes the indoors, TV, computer, reading	**indoor person**	5	**outdoor person**	*likes being outdoors*
wakes up easily at very slight sound	**light sleeper**	6	**heavy sleeper, sound sleeper**	*hard to wake up*
never late	**on time, punctual**	7	**often late**	*not on time, this is not polite*
ready anytime, no planning needed	**spontaneous**	8	**needs advance notice**	*needs to make preparations*
likes camping, hiking, fishing, campfires	**roughing it**	9	**likes the Hilton**	*likes the good life, comfort*
it's longer, but better views	**take the scenic route**	10	**A to B as fast as possible**	*in a hurry to get there*
takes minimum clothing, in one backpack	**travel light**	11	**pack everything**	*brings many things, just in case*
detail person who plans thoroughly	**well-organized**	12	**often lose things**	*not a detail person, loses things*

13. **three-day weekend** Fri, Sat, Sun, or Sat, Sun, Mon. *It was a three-day weekend, so we went camping.*
14. **airsick, seasick, carsick** to throw up food and drink because of the motion. *I got seasick on the cruise.*
15. **backpacking** travel with just a bag on your back. *We went backpacking. We backpacked all over Spain.*
16. **bumper-to-bumper** the traffic is very crowed, cars move very slowly. *The traffic was bumper-to-bumper.*
17. **commute** takes over 30 minutes to get there each way. *I commute to school. My commute is two hours.*
18. **city boy, country boy** knows and likes city life, likewise for the country. *My father is a country boy.*
19. **fall through, fell through** plans are canceled, ended. *Our plans fell through and we stayed home.*
20. **gap year** time off from school to travel, rest or work. *I took a gap year to travel in Europe.*
21. **hassle** takes long, is complicated, a bother. *It was a hassle to get a visa to go there.*
22. **happy camper** even though things are difficult or uncomfortable, they are happy. *She's a happy camper.*
23. **long lines** many people waiting, at a toll booth or park entrance. *There were long lines at every ride.*
24. **look forward to** to be happy about a future event. *I'm looking forward to this winter vacation.*
25. **lost** to not know where you are, need to ask directions. *We were lost. Honestly, my father gets lost a lot.*
26. **memories** things you remember. *I have great memories of that vacation. I have fond memories of Rome.*
27. **parade** lots of people or vehicles going through town and waving. *The lantern parade was very colorful.*
28. **peak time, peak season** popular time, very crowded. *It was peak time. I hate to travel during peak season.*
29. **rip off** the price is way too high, almost like stealing. *That place is a rip off. We got ripped off.*
30. **rush hour** cars very crowded on the streets, 8 - 9 a.m., and 5 - 6 p.m.
31. **scenic route** the long way, but lots of sightseeing. *We took the scenic route.*
32. **sightseeing** great things to look at. *We went sightseeing. There were lots of sights to see.*
33. **speeding ticket, speed limit** money penalty for going too fast.
34. **souvenir** you buy and bring it home from vacation *My mother collects souvenirs of every vacation.*
35. **stressed, stressed out, stressful** not fun. *I was stressed. I was stressed out. It was stressful.*

Vocabulary Buffet

36. **tentative plans** maybe, hopeful plans. *We have tentative plans to go camping, but it may rain.*
37. **toll booth, toll road** where they charge money to use the highway. A road that is not free.
38. **tourist trap** the only store in the area. It has no competition, so it charges high prices.
39. **tranquil** relaxing. *We stayed in a secluded cabin in the woods. It was quiet and tranquil.*

1. **The festival was:** exciting, thrilling, fantastic, well-organized, disorganized, over-priced, over-rated
2. **The ride was scary:** heart-pounding, exciting, thrilling, fantastic, awesome, expensive, reasonable
3. **The theme park was:** crowded, packed, so-so, awesome, thrilling, exciting, a-thrill-a-minute
4. **The lines were:** long, slow, short, fast, a one-hour wait, took forever
5. **The trip / the drive was:** boring, monotonous, scenic, long, too long, uneventful
6. **The traffic was:** slow, bumper to bumper, crawling, stop and go
7. **The weather was:** clear, crystal clear, hazy, cloudy, windy, hot, humid, muggy, cold, freezing

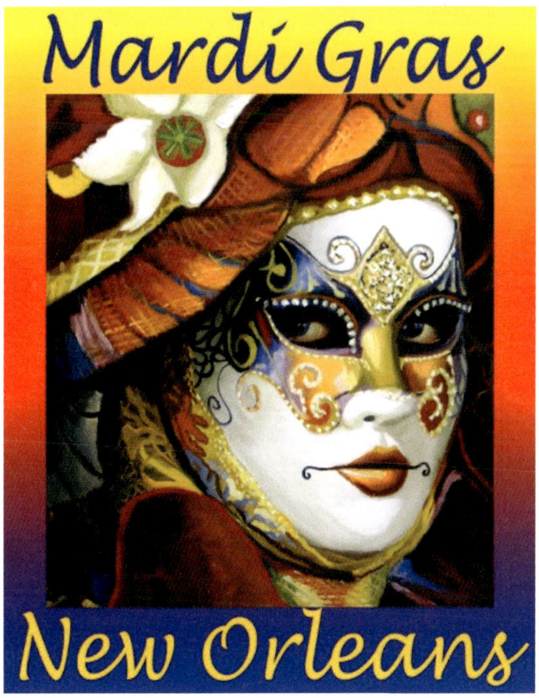

Vocabulary Check

You will hear a short sentence with three possible answers, A, B, C. Mark the best answer with a big, black dot.

	1	2	3	4	5	6	7	8	9	10
A	O	O	O	O	O	O	O	O	O	O
B	O	O	O	O	O	O	O	O	O	O
C	O	O	O	O	O	O	O	O	O	O

1 Take the quiz
2 Transcribe it
3 Check your answers

Longer Answers with Details

Focus! Make good, long sentences, and try to use some new vocabulary.

1. Longer writing is longer, smoother, and better speaking.
2. You have never said these things before, so read, record, and listen to yourself.

1 What was your favorite vacation ever? *How long did you stay? Did you ever go on a package tour?*

____

____

____

2 What festival or place is on your bucket list? *Why? What are your top three?*

____

____

____

3 Do you know your schedule for next semester? *Will you take a gap year? And do what?*

____

____

____

4 What will you do this semester break? *Will you have a part-time job?*

____

____

____

Answer in Academic Format

This will improve your speaking, essays, and presentations.

Answer in academic format. Use specific names of people, places, food, date, time.

1 Is your neighborhood happening or boring? ***Do you live in the city or on the outskirts?***

My neighborhood is definitely happening. I live near City University, and that is party central. ***First****, there's a lot of live music and performances every weekend. They even have jugglers and acrobats sometimes.* ***Second****, it's fashion town. There's lots of shops and boutiques that cater to college kids.* ***Third****, there are restaurants and foods from all over the world. My favorite is Thai food, for example, tom-yum-goong, which is spicy shrimp.*

____

____

____

____

2 What three things did you learn this semester?

This semester was an eye-opener. ***First****, I learned that I am no longer the smartest kid in class. In high school, I was pretty much the smartest one in class. Here, EVERYBODY was the smartest in their high school class. It's very competitive.* ***Second****, I learned to prioritize: determine what is most important and do that first.* ***Third****, I learned to be more friendly and helpful. Every time I helped one classmate, two or three helped me.*

____

____

____

____

For example? What about you?

Pronunciation Practice

Did you make an audio of this in unit 1? Great. Go back and listen to it. *You can hear your improvement.*

i	æ	ɛ	ɪ
eat	at	et	it
he'd	had	head	hid
deed	dad	dead	did
neat	nat	net	knit
peet	pat	pet	pit
reed	rad	red	rid

L	R	N	W
life	rife	knife	wife
led	red	Ned	wed
leer	rear	near	we're
len	ren	nen	when
leak	reek	neek	weak
leel	real	kneel	wheel

G, J	Ch	Z	Sh	S
Jane	chain	Zane	Shane	sane
jew	chew	zoo	shoe	Sue
Joe	cho	Zoh	show	so
gin	chin	Zen	shin	sin
gyp	chip	zip	ship	sip
Jack	chak	Zak	shack	sack

Descriptive Paragraph

Include a photo, and triple extra points if you're in the photo!

Answer any question in the unit: Vacations, festivals, holidays, transportation.

For example: ***How's your transportation life?***

During the week, my transportation life is long. I live ***on the outskirts of town,*** *and I have a three-hour* ***commute*** *each day. And every day it's at* ***rush hour****. My first class is at 9:00 and my last class is at 5:00. I take the subway, line number four, and luckily I don't have any* ***transfers****. I live near* ***the end of the line*** *so I can usually get a seat in the morning. On the weekends I usually* ***hang out*** *in my neighborhood. For any other travel, I take a city bus. It's much* ***less stressful*** *than the subway, and I can always sit down.*

The good news about living on the ***outskirts*** *is that it's easy to get out of town on the weekends. However, sometimes coming back to town on Sunday evening, the traffic is* ***bumper to bumper.*** *My father is a* ***country boy*** *at heart, and he likes to get out of town every chance he gets. We have a big* ***SUV,*** *so it's pretty* ***convenient*** *to travel. And he always takes the long,* ***scenic route****. We* ***get lost*** *every now and then, but my father says that's part of the adventure! Actually, I think he pretends to be lost sometimes. I mean, he's got a* ***GPS*** *in the car and on his phone. Anyway. He's an* ***action addict, adrenaline junkie****. He likes the great outdoors. He likes* ***roughing it****, and mom goes along, reluctantly. My parents really* ***look forward to*** *the weekends. My father likes to plan things down to the last detail, but my mom is more* ***spontaneous****. She tells him "We're going to the woods. The bears don't care, let's go!" I usually* ***ride shotgun*** *and he makes me the* ***navigator****. I watch the* ***GPS*** *and tell him when and where to turn. When it's* ***peak season*** *or holidays, he likes to leave at the* ***crack of dawn*** *to beat the traffic. He likes to* ***travel light****, so if we need anything we just pick it up on the way. My parents both work very hard during the week, so I think getting away on the weekends is their way of making sure our family gets enough* ***quality time****.*

TOEFL Essay

Answer a conversation question with a TOEFL essay. You know the drill.

Write about what interests you. Use any question in this unit. Below are other possibilities.

1. What's your favorite festival, theme park, or vacation, and three reasons why. Or, what are your three favorites?
2. What was your favorite vacation, or your three favorite?
3. Is your family the outdoors type? Prove it.

A15 Amy Lawrence

What's your favorite festival, theme park, or vacation?

I love theme parks and festivals. They are like mini-vacations. Luckily, my parents like them also, or most likely, I got my love from them. My parents are the outdoors type, especially my father. He's ***good to go*** any time, any where. My favorite theme park is *Everland*, my favorite festival is the *Jindo Sea Parting Festival,* and the festival that's on my ***bucket list*** is *Mardi Gras* in New Orleans.

First, *Everland* has so much to do and see. Specifically, it has a Global Fair with shops and ***souvenirs*** from all around the world. Also, *Zootopia* is, well, a zoo, that has all kinds of animals. My mom does not like pets so I appreciate being around the animals there. The *European Adventure* has ***authentic*** (I think) restaurants. My favorite part of everything there is the roller coasters. Whoa! After my first ride, I was ***hooked***. I'm ***addicted*** now.

Second, my favorite festival is the *Jindo Sea Parting*. That is so cool. My father's hometown is near there so we just stay at my grandparents. My father ***is into*** festivals. He wants us to understand and ***appreciate*** Korean culture, so we have been to about every festival in Korea. We go in the spring when the sea parts and the weather is great. I especially like being able to see all the stars at night, which you cannot see from a big city. It's a great ***family atmosphere*** there.

Third, my middle school teacher got her master's degree in New Orleans, and she loved the place. Her ***eyes would light up*** when she talked about *Mardi Gras*. That's French for 'Fat Tuesday.' Basically, it means that people would pig out on Tuesday, because the Catholic season of Lent started the next day, and so Tuesday was their last day of partying. Also, they have these huge ***parades*** where people on the floats throw big necklace beads and toys to you. If you yell enough at them.

I guess I get the love of traveling and festivals from my parents. They are kind of traditional and like traditional festivals. They buy antique souvenirs wherever we go and mom ***displays*** them on a shelf in the living room. On another wall, she has photos of our travels. Everland has the most photos because we go there often. Jindo is just so neat because of the ***natural phenomenon*** of the sea parting, and Mardi Gras is on my list because my teacher ***infected me with enthusiasm*** for it. The only ***cure*** is to go there. (420 words)

Zoo at Everland

Sea parting at Jindo

Parade at Mardi Gras

Do it.
Get it over with and
go meet your friends.

Hey! You can practice outside.

Hey! Go back and listen to your first recording.
You can hear your progress.

WRAP PARTY!

PERSONALITY	FESTIVALS	SCHOOL	TRAVEL
Is your father, mother a light sleeper or a sound sleeper? *For example?*	**What's your favorite festival?** *Why? How many times have you been?*	**Did you go to MT this semester?** *When? Where? Did you make any new friends?*	**Do you have a driver's license?** *How often do you drive?*
Do your parents like roughing it or staying at the Hilton?	**What's your favorite vacation souvenir?** *How much did it cost?*	**What was your hardest class this semester?** *Your easiest?*	**Will you ever take a gap year to travel?** *Where to? When?*
Does your father take the scenic route, or gets there as fast as possible?	**Are your family trips well-organized or kind of chaotic?** *For example?*	**Are your grades better this semester than last semester?** *What happened?*	**What's the longest car trip you ever took?** *Who all went?*
Does your mother travel light, or does she bring everything?	**Did you ever get ripped off while on vacation?** *Did you ever lose something? Have something stolen?*	**Did you make any new friends this semester?** *Did you make any enemies?*	**Did your father ever get a speeding ticket?** *What did your mom say?*
Would you rather go to a water park or a snow festival?	**Did you ever fall asleep on the subway and miss your stop?** *Was drinking involved?*	**Did you join any clubs this semester?** *Were you ever rejected from joining a club?*	**When flying, do you prefer a window seat or aisle seat?** *Front or back of the plane?*

TRIVIA CONTEST!
Name 10 countries that end 'ia'.

1. Russia
2. ______
3. ______
4. ______
5. ______
6. ______
7. ______
8. ______
9. ______
10. ______

One extra point for each country you have been to.

For example? When? Who? How long? What about you?

What's your favorite theme park?

PERSONALITY	FESTIVALS	SCHOOL	TRAVEL
Is your father, mother an early bird or a night owl? *For example?*	**Does your father like the outdoors, or is he a city boy?** *For example?*	**What BIG thing did you learn this semester?** *Will you do better next semester?*	**When your father drives, does he have a lot of patience or a short fuse?**
Would you rather go to a concert or a ball game?	**What's your favorite theme park?** *How many times have you been there?*	**If you could do one thing over this semester, what would it be?**	**What's the longest flight you ever took?** *Can you sleep on a plane?*
Do you prefer winter or summer vacations? *For example?*	**What's the wildest ride you have ever been on?** *Do you like scary rides?*	**What's your dream job? What's your plan B?** *What will you probably do?*	**How do you get to school?** *How much do you spend per week on transportation?*
On vacation, is your father cheap or a big spender *For example?*	**Did you ever go white-water rafting?** *Camping overnight?*	**Do you like your major?** *If you could change your major, what would it be?*	**How does your father get to work? Mother?** *How long does it take?*
Are your family trips well-organized or kind of chaotic? *For example?*	**Have you seen any big fireworks?** *When? Who did you go with?*	**Do you know your courses for next semester?**	**Were you ever in a traffic accident?** *Was it your fault?*

If you were stuck on an island for a month, what 10 things would you pack?

Ex. *sunglasses*

1. ______
2. ______
3. ______
4. ______
5. ______
6. ______
7. ______
8. ______
9. ______
10. ______

For example? When? Who? How long? What about you?

PACIFIC OCEAN
CANADA
MEXICO
BRITISH COLUMBIA
ALBERTA
SASKATCHEWAN
MANITOBA
WASHINGTON
OREGON
IDAHO
MONTANA
WYOMING
NORTH DAKOTA
SOUTH DAKOTA
NEBRASKA
KANSAS
COLORADO
UTAH
NEVADA
CALIFORNIA
ARIZONA
NEW MEXICO
TEXAS
OKLAHOMA
SONORA
CHIHUAHUA
COAHUILA
DURANGO
BAJA CALIFORNIA
BAJA CALIFORNIA SUR
Golfo de California
Rocky Mts.
Great Basin
Colorado Plateau
Llano Estacado
Edwards Plateau
Bolsón de Mapimí
Sonoran Desert
Mojave Desert
Great Salt Lake
Coast Ranges
Sierra Nevada
Cascade Range
Channel Islands
Guadalupe (Mex.)
VANCOUVER
Victoria
Calgary
Lethbridge
Medicine Hat
Swift Current
Moose Jaw
Regina
Brandon
Portage La Prairie
SEATTLE
Tacoma
Olympia
Spokane
Yakima
PORTLAND
Salem
Eugene
Boise
Pocatello
Idaho Falls
Missoula
Helena
Great Falls
Butte
Billings
Bismarck
Rapid City
Casper
Cheyenne
SALT LAKE CITY
Ogden
Provo
DENVER
Boulder
Colorado Springs
Pueblo
Grand Junction
Las Vegas
Reno
Carson City
SACRAMENTO
SAN FRANCISCO
Oakland
San Jose
Fresno
Bakersfield
LOS ANGELES
Long Beach
Anaheim
San Bernardino
SAN DIEGO
Tijuana
Mexicali
Ensenada
PHOENIX
Mesa
Tucson
Flagstaff
Albuquerque
Santa Fe
El Paso
Ciudad Juárez
Chihuahua
Hermosillo
Ciudad Obregón
Los Mochis
Amarillo
Lubbock
Midland
Odessa
Abilene
Fort Worth
Austin
San Antonio
Corpus Christi
Laredo
Nuevo Laredo
Monterrey
Monclova
Torreón
Wichita Falls
Yuma
Mt. Rainier 4392
Mt. Hood 3424
Mt. Shasta 4317
Mt. Whitney 4418
Pikes Pk. 4301
Mt. Elbert 4399
Grand Teton 4197
YELLOWSTONE NATIONAL PARK
GRAND CANYON NATIONAL PARK
YOSEMITE NATIONAL PARK
GLACIER NAT. PARK

Have you ever been to the USA?

Where? When? Why? Who? How? How long?

Where was your favorite? Why? How was the food?

Any place in the states on your bucket list?

Have you ever traveled abroad? What place is on your bucket list?

Where? When? Why? Who? How? How long? How was the food?

Vocabulary Index

If you want more information about a vocabulary or idiom, look it up at: dictionary. com

After every unit, highlight the vocabulary you learned.

After every conversation test, highlight the vocabulary you used.

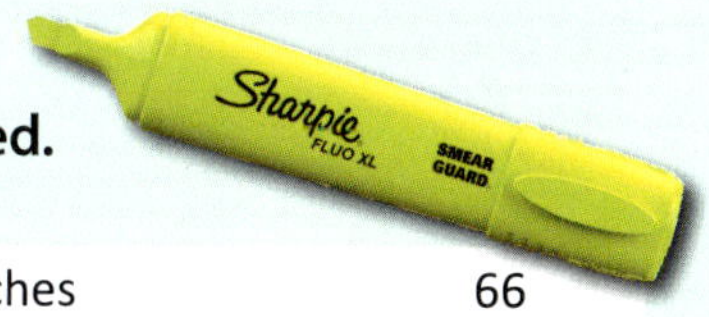

Audio File Library

Scan the QR code to go to the page-by-page audio files web page.

Each unit contains about 30 minutes of audio. A total of about 3 hours for the whole book.
The audios range in length from 1 to 3 minutes. Easy. You can transcribe each Quiz in about 10 minutes.
Playing computer games or watching YouTube for 3 hours will not change your life. These audio files will.

INSTRUCTIONS

Every time you listen to an audio file, highlight the page number with yellow.
Every time you record and listen to yourself, highlight it again with orange, green, blue or purple.

	Unit 1	2	3	4	5	6
1 Engaging Activity	Page 14	26	38	50	62	74
2 Conversation Preparation	15	27	39	51	63	75
3 Basic Conversations	16	28	40	52	64	76
4 Basic Conversations	17	29	41	53	65	77
5 Vocabulary	18	30	42	54	66	78
6 Vocabulary Quiz	19	31	43	55	67	79
7 Longer Answers with Details	20	32	44	56	68	80
8 Academic Answers	21	33	45	57	69	81
8 Pronunciation Practice	21	33	45	57	69	81
9 Descriptive Paragraph	22	34	46	58	70	82
10 TOEFL Essay	23	35	47	59	71	83
11 Wrap Party	24	36	48	60	72	84
12 Wrap Party	25	37	49	61	73	85
Quiz score						
How long it took to transcribe						

DETAILS

1. Do a voice check. Record yourself describing what you did last weekend. See how you really sound. ***Save it.***
2. Listen, repeat, and record every audio file. Several times. Listen to what you sound like.
3. After every unit, go back and listen to your very first audio. Play it. Hear your improvement.
4. Save all your recordings in one folder. That will be an album where you can track your progress.
5. Later, you can go back and listen to how you sounded on the first day. You'll hear your improvement.

You're in a race against time.

The older you get the harder it is to master speaking.
You can cram grammar and test preparation books all you want later.

Questions?

THE CLASS

1 ***What if students are low-level speakers? Can they handle this?***
Yes. Absolutely. They write what they will say, ***My father is a teacher*** and then say it in class. Speaking ability is not improved by listening to a teacher talk about the English language.

2 ***What if they don't do the homework?***
They make an **F**. This is a required course. Homework takes 30 minutes, and they are writing about themselves. Simple. They do homework in other classes. *What's the problem?*

3 ***What about instructions?***
They're on video. Also, pre-class instructions and post-class feedback are sent by email or uploaded on the website. If students can read and hear it at home, teachers shouldn't say it in class.

4 ***What does the teacher do in class?***
As little as possible. If the teacher is talking, students are not. Students improve when *students* are talking. This is a new world with new technology. Input at home, output in class. *Simple.*

5 ***Are big classes really better?***
Absolutely. More partners = more variety = more repetition = more improvement.
Big classes have more partners of similar ability. **Big classes have more energy.**

THE TEST

1 ***Is transcribing difficult?***
No. Low-level speakers speak at a low level. They're transcribing what THEY said. ***I'm born in Seoul.*** They're not transcribing the **BBC News**.

2 ***How long does it take to transcribe?***
It takes everybody about two hours. There is a YIN and YANG. The better speakers speak more and have more transcribing ability. The lesser speakers speak less, and have less to transcribe.

3 ***What if students aren't good at MS Word?***
They soon will be. MS Word is an academic, and real-world skill. They will not get a job without it. If they have to learn it in this class, they will. Besides, they're given a template, they just type. *Simple.*

4 ***What about feedback and error correction?***
Students hear and read their own mistakes when they transcribe, and then fix their top 5 mistakes. If they can tie their own shoes, they can find their own mistakes: *When I was a middle school.*

5 ***Does speaking really improve 50%?***
Actually, it's usually more, about 70%. When a student goes from *My hometown is Busan*, (4 words) to *My hometown is Busan. I lived there until I was eight.* (11 words), that's a 175% increase.

Conversation Based
LEARNING
• PUBLISHING COMPANY •
Because life is not a grammar test

Jangchungdan-ro 8-gil 59-22, Jung-gu, Seoul, Korea 04614
PlanGBro@gmail.com • ConversationBasedLearning.com

Published and printed in South Korea, 2020

ISBN: 979-11-88562-06-0

Editors: Sarah Weeks, Sam Smith, and Stephanie Ptak
Design & Layout: Gunther Breaux
Photo credits: ©Bigstock, ©Gunther Breaux

ACKNOWLEDGEMENTS

Amy Aleha's audio recording contribution is greatly appreciated. She makes this book possible.

I would like to thank: Sean Dailey, Sarah Weeks, Stephanie Ptak, Sam Smith, Shaun Manning, Jim Hwang, Jim Life, Rhea Metituk, Kinga Szilagyi, and Daniel Deacon who gave me the great benefits of their experience and expertise. Sean Dailey's help and contribution to the audio are greatly appreciated.

Gui Lim Kang's help in design and teaching methodology has enhanced this work.

Gunther Breaux has taught English Conversation to university students in Korea for 23 years. He also taught Business English at the Korea Development Institute (KDI) Graduate School of Public Policy and Management, and Computer Graphics at the Korea National University of the Arts. He's presented at international conferences in Korea, Japan, China, Thailand, and the United States. His original thought and contribution to English Education is Conversation-Based Learning.

He has a BA in Advertising Design, an MA in American History, and an MATESOL. Before Korea, Gunther's job history included commercial artist, art director at an advertising agency, bartender, dancing instructor, diver, welder and tugboat captain. He has run five full marathons and has a black belt in Taekwondo. He's an interesting guy who knows the value of interesting teaching materials. He also knows that life is a contest of passion and ability. His books give you the ability to express your passion, in English.

For more books by Gunther Breaux go to: **ConversationBasedLearning.com**

Contact the author: **PlanGBro@gmail.com**

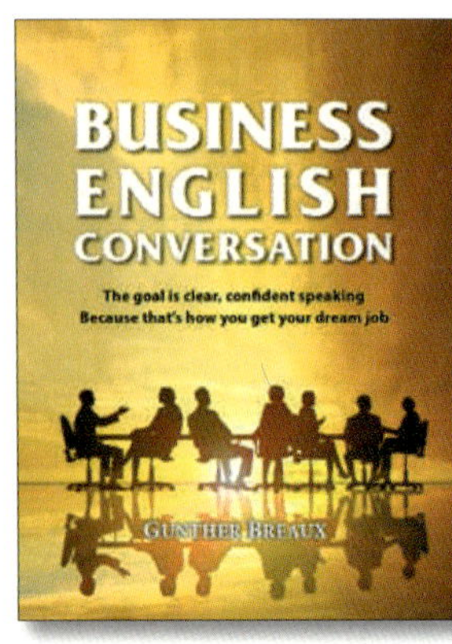